Doing Justice in Our Cities

*Lessons in Public Policy
from America's Heartland*

Warren R. Copeland

WESTMINSTER
JOHN KNOX PRESS
LOUISVILLE · KENTUCKY

© 2009 Warren R. Copeland

First edition
Published by Westminster John Knox Press
Louisville, Kentucky

09 10 11 12 13 14 15 16 17 18—10 9 8 7 6 5 4 3 2 1

Portions of chapter 9 were originally published as "Politics as an Act of Faith" in *Belonging Together: Faith and Politics in a Relational World.* Ed. Douglas Sturm (Claremont, CA: P&F Press, 2003).

Book design by Sharon Adams
Cover design by designpointinc.com

Library of Congress Cataloging-in-Publication Data

Copeland, Warren R.
    Doing justice in our cities : lessons in public policy from America's heartland /
Warren Copeland.
        p. cm.
    Includes bibliographical references and index.
    ISBN 978-0-664-23229-0 (alk. paper)
    1. Cities and towns—Religious aspects—Christianity.   2. Springfield (Ohio)—Case studies.
3. Policy sciences.   4. Church and social problems.   5. Social ethics.   I. Title.
    BR115.C45C67   2009
    261.809771'49—dc22

                                                                    2009001919

PRINTED IN THE UNITED STATES OF AMERICA

♾ The paper used in this publication meets the minimum requirements
of the American National Standard for Information Sciences—Permanence of Paper
for Printed Library Materials, ANSI Z39.48-1992.

Westminster John Knox Press advocates the responsible use of our natural resources.
The text paper of this book is made from at least 30% post-consumer waste.

For Angel, Megan, Tracey, Brianna, Tommy, and Allison,
our grandchildren who live the diversity that is the promise of our cities.

Contents

Acknowledgments

No work is the product of a single person, but this volume draws upon the work and experience of others by its very nature. To a significant extent it is about public action; public action is people acting together. I am deeply grateful to all of those inside and outside of government with whom I have acted here in Springfield, Ohio, over the past twenty years. I am particularly indebted to my colleagues on the Springfield City Commission, whether we have always agreed or not, for their willingness to join with me in public action. I am deeply grateful to the city staff who work so diligently with so little positive public recognition. Among them I must single out Matt Kridler; he is simply the best administrative leader I have ever known. In the final analysis, my most important public colleagues are the citizens of Springfield who in the face of the decline of industrial America have struggled so hard to create a liveable future for this community we love.

I also live in an academic community that has shared in this project. Most immediately, the urban studies faculty of Wittenberg University has provided a place to consider the issues discussed here and a workforce to produce analyses of Springfield and to relate them to other cities. In particular, Jeff Ankrom pulled together the lion's share of the data about Springfield I use here and is my most consistent sounding board about it. The Social Ethics Seminar remains my most important support as a religious ethicist. They devoted a large portion of the program of their annual meeting in 2006 to discussion and constructive criticism of this work. Among the members of the seminar, I must mention Roger Hatch, who not only helped me figure out how to organize my thoughts but also read the entire manuscript more than once, offering invaluable editorial suggestions. Friends and colleagues like Jeff and Roger are hard to find and wonderful to have. It has been a genuine pleasure to add David Rusk to these intellectual colleagues in recent years. As will be obvious, I have learned a lot by reading

David's work, but I have come to know him as a kindred spirit in the struggle for the future of our cities.

Thankfully, my wife Clara does not want to be a political wife, although she would be a great one. However, I have never doubted that she believed deeply in what I have been doing in my public life, almost as deeply as in her own work as a kindergarten teacher who mixes care and competence to make a real difference in the lives of her children. I have learned so much about life in a city through the experiences of our children and have a gained a new sense of urgency about the future of our cities from our grandchildren. May we all continue to think and act to create the cities that our children and grandchildren need and deserve.

To all of those I have mentioned and all of those I did not have room to mention, I am grateful for your help and support. For any errors I have made here, I alone take responsibility.

Introduction

In the time I have served as mayor of Springfield, Ohio, there has been one question that I have not wanted to hear: "Is mayor a full-time job?" Perhaps I should just say "yes"; some weeks that is close to true. But I usually say "no." So begins a string of questions that I doubt helps my credibility with the questioner. "What is your full-time job?" "I am a college professor." Now there is one big step out of reality to the average questioner. "What do you teach?" "I teach religion." I take another big step away from reality for most people. "What kind of religion do you teach?" "I teach social ethics." Usually that ends the conversation and my credibility as a practical politician. So I hate to hear that first question: "Is mayor a full-time job?"

The only time I can remember wearing a tuxedo for anything other than a wedding was for the original dedication of the Springfield Inn. Among other things, that tells you something about just how much of a social animal I am. That dedication marked the culmination of a lot of hard work by a number of people to bring a downtown hotel back to Springfield. At the reception before the dinner, Richard Kuss invited Clara and me to join his table for dinner. Dick Kuss is the former CEO of Springfield's Bonded Oil, which became Emro Marketing and is now Speedway/SuperAmerica—owners and operators of gas stations. Dick is one of the truly nicest persons I have ever known, but I have learned that his genuine niceness is usually joined to a practical purpose. Later when we gathered around Dick's table for dinner, we were introduced to the then-president of the Credit Life Insurance Company. Sent down from the parent company in Chicago, this young man on the rise and his wife had decided to live in Dublin, Ohio, an exclusive suburb of Columbus. Dick was looking for ways to connect them more to Springfield. We had not been settled very long before this young man, who could help or hurt Springfield, turned to me and asked, "Is mayor a full-time job?" "No." "What is your full-time job?" "I am a college professor." "What do you teach?" "I teach religion." "What kind of religion do you teach?" "I teach social ethics." I doubt that this is what Dick had in mind for this conversation.

"Well, tell me, Mayor, what do you think are the three most important ethical issues facing America today?" Now there was a new twist, but not one that was likely to work out well. Should I be honest or try to bend the conversation to the reasons that Springfield was such a good place for an insurance company to do business? Rightly or wrongly, I thought I felt Dick Kuss squirming across the table. I am usually too candid, and I certainly was that night. "The issue that worries me the most is the increasing number of children who are growing up poor. They are not getting the education they need to be employed as adults at wages high enough for them to support a family in the new job market that requires more education all the time." That response ended that conversation as the young insurance executive decided to talk to others about more comfortable topics. The Springfield banker sitting next to me wanted to talk more about poor children, and we had a very good conversation. I am sure that this was not what Dick hoped would happen that evening. A year or so later Credit Life Insurance closed its Springfield operation and moved the jobs that remained to Chicago. I count it an act of grace that Dick has still supported me over the years, and we have done some good things together.

Yes, I am a professor of social ethics in the Religion Department of Wittenberg University and the mayor of Springfield, Ohio. Springfield is a very typical city of the industrial Midwest, with all of the problems of race, poverty, crime, older neighborhoods, and suburbanization. That is why *Newsweek* chose to focus its entire fiftieth anniversary issue on Springfield.[1] They could study the status of the American Dream in all of America through Springfield because we were so typical. For the same reason, major media like the *New York Times* or *Washington Post* or CNN choose Springfield and Clark County as the place to find out what is happening in the industrial heartland during presidential campaigns. When the British paper *The Guardian* decided to run a contest to see which of its readers could write the best letters to influence American voters in 2004, they chose Springfield and Clark County residents. Being typical is not necessarily good. It means that Springfield has all of the problems common to contemporary American cities: violent crime, drug abuse, poverty, troubled family lives, and loss of well-paying jobs. Yet we can take a certain pride in being typical. *Newsweek* found here "that stubborn American grit in adversity"[2] that refuses to give up on the dream of a better life. On the plus side, Springfield's size (approximately sixty-five thousand) provides a manageable microcosm of cities much larger. We in the Urban Studies Program at Wittenberg claim that Springfield is an ideal place to study cities because it is a real city but also is small enough to get our minds around. We actually believe that claim. As the director of the Urban Studies Program at Wittenberg, I have participated in a significant amount of research and analysis of Springfield based upon theories about U.S. cities generally. Springfield fits those theories all too well.

I bring a particular perspective to these urban studies analyses. I learned the practice of religious social ethics from the Ethics and Society Field of the University of Chicago Divinity School between 1968 and 1973. Specifically, I learned how to recognize issues of injustice in our social order, to identify alternative perspectives on those issues of injustice, to analyze how those perspectives arose out of different assumptions about human meaning, and to propose ways of expanding justice that adequately take account of human meaning.[3] What does that sentence actually mean? I hope two examples help. In my book on poverty and welfare, I described the issue of poverty in the United States; looked at four very different positions on poverty and welfare; examined how each of these positions understood the principles of individuality, community, worth, motivation, and hope; developed theologically grounded views of each of these five principles; and then laid out guidelines for welfare reform based upon these views. In a course on racism that I have taught at Wittenberg since 1977, we examine the history of race in the United States and the tension between racial identity and self-determination (e.g., Malcolm X) and integration into an interracial society (e.g., Martin Luther King) that has been a constant in attempts to address it. We try to understand how each approach is rooted in fundamental aspects of what it means to be human and then think about what sort of society would try to make both possible. I guess it was inevitable that I would analyze my experience in city government in a similar way.

Finally, I assume that the drive to think about injustice and how to overcome it arises from faith. Specifically, I am a Christian for whom public action is a central aspect of my faith. For me, the struggle for social justice is not just a way to express my faith, but it is also a place to find my faith and test it. So I heard the call I received asking whether I would be willing to serve on the Springfield City Commission as fundamentally a call from God to consider a new way to live my faith. This lies at the core of who I am and what I do. I will ask the reader to think about this faith issue a lot more after I have described the injustice that is metropolitan America today and analyzed some alternative ways of looking at it.

In the weeks following the 2004 presidential election, a map of the United States appeared in *USA Today* and was circulated among conservative talk shows that showed all of the counties that had voted for George W. Bush in red and all of the counties that had voted for John Kerry in blue. There were a lot of red and some dots of blue surrounded by red, suggesting that the United States had turned red—that is, Republican. Some scholars at the University of Michigan circulated some maps that suggested otherwise.[4] In one map they simply changed the size of the red and blue areas to reflect the population of the counties. The amount of red and blue was now about as equal as the election was. They then produced a map that had shades of purple that identified counties that only leaned red or blue with size adjusted for population. The result was a map that was mostly shades of purple. Whatever the original map may say about our politics, it was profoundly anticity. In it cities became just small blue dots in a red ocean.

This is not a strictly partisan matter. Most Democratic strategists believe that most statewide and national elections are now won and lost in the suburbs, so they are reluctant to draw attention to urban issues. They certainly do not want their candidates to be too closely identified with cities and their problems. When President Bush announced his budget in February 2005, this anticity bias became even clearer. The cuts in federal programs came down most heavily upon cities already suffering from a loss of jobs and population. What we saw so starkly visible in the television reports from New Orleans immediately after Hurricane Katrina was the neglect of our cities. Nearly any American city that gave a simple order to its citizens to evacuate would produce similar pictures. Those without resources would be left behind. This neglect was made even more tragic by the fact that so many of us had ignored the problem for so long as to believe that it did not exist. Once upon a time, cities were seen as the birthplaces of civilization and democracy; now they are seen as centers of crime and deterioration. I believe that the tendency to withdraw from cities and let them decline is a profoundly destructive force in our society. I also consider it a fundamental ethical issue for our citizens and a critical religious issue for people of faith.

In the first section of this book, I tell the story about how I got into urban politics in Springfield and how that career has introduced me to the challenge of urban life at the beginning of the twenty-first century. This section will include a heavy dose of our guru, David Rusk, who helped us think about our situation and what to do about it. Along the way and in parts 2 and 3 also, I try to add two sorts of reflections upon the narrative. I indicate where I think our experience raises ethical and religious issues and how events in Springfield are typical of American cities. This narrative section describes the dynamics of my engagement in public life in Springfield, Ohio, and in the process describes the issue of justice central to contemporary urban life in the United States. The division between cities and their suburbs starves city governments and distributes opportunity for their citizens in ways that are fundamentally unjust.

In the second part of the book, I analyze the ethical landscape of actors within American cities and explore my own religious and theological resources for thinking about justice in cities. These reflections arise out of the context established in the first section of the book; that context raises the questions about which I reflect. In the process, I identify and illustrate a variety of ways of looking at cities. Then, I seek to bring aspects of my religious experience and theological analysis that speak to the questions posed by my experience to bear on central issues facing cities. Along the way, I argue for real diversity not as a currently popular slogan but as the fundamental human value appropriate to guide action to address metropolitan justice. Diversity is the challenge and the gift that cities offer us today.

In the third and final part of the book, I explore where we need to go if we are to answer that challenge and receive that gift. The outside game of dispersing poverty and sharing revenue on a metropolitan basis is essential, and Springfield has pursued it strongly in recent years. I also describe the inside-game efforts that we are in the midst of now to retain and attract middle- and upper-income residents.[5] This attempt to project into the future is informed by the ethical, religious, and theological reflections in the second part of the book that in turn arise out of the context described in the first part of the book.

That explanation of the flow of this book sounded a lot more theoretical than I intended. I understand general principles best by seeing real examples of them. So I shall season this entire discussion with very specific examples from my experience, mostly with the place and people I know and love: Springfield, Ohio. I do this in part out of the conviction that lived experiences are the reality those principles must help us understand and shape. However, I continually point out how those Springfield illustrations are typical of what other cities face and of more general ethical and religious issues. Welcome to my world of urban politics as an ethical and religious challenge. I hope that I can help make it your world, too.

PART ONE
LIVED EXPERIENCE

Chapter 1

The Call

A Professor Becomes a Politician

"I guess you know why I am calling." It was September 1988. On the other end of the line was Wes Babian, the minister of First Baptist Church. I had no clue why Wes was calling. "Tim Ayers asked me to see if you might be interested in serving on the city commission." Now there was a good question I had never asked myself. "I honestly do not know, but I am willing to think about it. Let me talk to Clara and get back to you," I told Wes. Tim Ayers was the mayor of Springfield, Ohio, in 1988. He had spoken about the city at First Baptist Church as a part of our Lenten series. As is my tendency, I was outspoken about something or other and attracted Tim's attention. Jack Blackburn had recently resigned from the Springfield City Commission—only the most recent loss to a city government in crisis. The city commission had to appoint a replacement, and various members were looking for candidates. To understand my ultimate answer to Tim, it may help you to know more about both Springfield and about me.

WHO IS SPRINGFIELD?

Someone new to Springfield quickly learns that this is a city whose past hangs heavily over its present. A permanent settlement was established at Springfield,

Ohio, in 1799.[1] By 1818, it became the county seat for the newly created Clark County. In the 1830s, the national road (now U.S. 40) extended to Springfield and for a time literally ended in Springfield. However, the city's heyday was between the Civil War and the Great Depression. Even now I am reminded quite often that at one time Springfield was home to the second-largest factory complex in the world. Only the Krupp factories in Germany were larger than the East Street Shops in Springfield. They were but a part of what made Springfield the farm implement capital of America. The owner of the East Street Works went broke in 1887. Other farm implement companies continued and in time were absorbed into International Harvester. Magazines published by one farm implement company evolved into the Crowell Publishing Company. By 1880, *Farm and Fireside* was very successful. *Woman's Home Companion* was acquired and also became very popular. In time, Crowell-Collier also acquired the *American* and *Collier's*. Add a number of smaller manufacturers to the farm implement and publishing giants, and you have a bustling midwestern industrial city. By 1920, Springfield bragged that it was "the best 60,000-resident city in the western hemisphere."[2]

The East Street Works burned down in 1902. As part of an antitrust agreement, International Harvester discontinued production of farm implements in Springfield, leaving behind its truck production.[3] A much smaller International Truck and Engine remains today the best-paying large manufacturer in the area. Crowell-Collier closed suddenly just before Christmas in 1956. In the 1970s and 1980s, people still talked about this event as though it had happened the week before. For many, it was the beginning of the decline of Springfield.

Developments outside the city limits also affected the city. In the 1960s, International Harvester built a large new assembly plant north of Springfield. Other industries moved out, leaving behind many vacant old factory buildings along the railroad tracks on the east and west sides. The opening of the Upper Valley Mall to the west of town in 1971 helped speed up the decline of downtown Springfield. Local voters approved an increase in the municipal income tax to 2 percent in return for a phase-out of property taxes for city government. Part of the additional tax revenue was used to acquire land in the core block of the city, to demolish the structures that were there, and to build a new city hall and other new buildings. By 1977, when I interviewed for a job at Wittenberg University, Springfield had the look of a worn, old industrial city with a hole in the ground downtown where the garage under city hall was to be built. Later we learned that locals loved to talk about the glorious past, usually as a part of criticizing their present and fearing their future.

During the spring of 1977, we came for a few days to find a new home. After looking at homes on the Northside for a day, we saw some homes in the multiple listing book on the Eastside, Westside, and especially the Southside of town that looked like what we wanted at a price we could manage. With some exceptions, north is where people with more money live and south is where those with less money live—which means that African Americans and poor whites, many with roots somewhere in Appalachia, are concentrated on the Southside. The largely white, blue-collar Eastside and Westside are left out of this too-simple north-south equation, and they do feel left out.

Our real estate agent suggested that we drive around the neighborhoods the next day before we picked up keys for the houses. In retrospect, it is clear that he wanted us to see that the southside homes were in racially mixed neighbor-hoods. We got the keys and have loved the house at 1613 Wittenberg Boulevard West ever since. We had no idea how dramatically we had just located ourselves in Springfield, Ohio. North is north, and south is south. Almost by accident, we had taken our stand on one side of that dividing line. As I became active in citywide school issues, I found that Northsiders were constantly surprised by Southside anger. We Southsiders were not. This kind of racial and economic geography makes Springfield a very typical American city with its full share of income and racial divisions.

The arrival of the Copelands did not turn Springfield around. In fact, things grew worse in the late 1970s and especially in the 1980s. A very ugly strike at International Harvester in 1979 tore the city apart.[4] The most positive news was defensive. In 1982, Springfield won a battle with Fort Wayne, Indiana, to be the primary location where International Harvester assembled International Harvester trucks.[5] Springfield's status as an extremely typical city led *Newsweek* to choose it as the hometown the magazine analyzed for its fiftieth anniversary issue in 1983. Some locals preferred to think that Springfield was chosen as a model city. However, *Newsweek* made clear that it liked Springfield for its problems as much as its successes. *Newsweek*'s story was about a community and five particular families enduring hard times. Their writers summarized, "There is a deep undercurrent of apprehension in Springfield's view of the future . . . exacerbated by a mistrust in the honesty and the competence of government."[6] *Newsweek* concluded that the American Dream had survived in Springfield, but they seemed a bit surprised that it had.

If anything, city government fared even worse than the city itself. The core problem was money. The economic decline of the city meant less revenue for city government. The inflation and recessions that hit the entire country were hardest on the industrial Midwest and especially on cities just like Springfield. The largest single blow was the loss of federal revenue-sharing funds in the early 1980s, $2 million that Springfield had put right in the middle of its general fund to pay fire and police salaries. These financial problems led city government to desperate measures that only seemed to make things worse. Voters raised the income tax to 2.5 percent for three years. When that increase came up for renewal, city government threatened to turn off two-thirds of the streetlights if it failed. It did fail, and the lights went out. In an effort to shift costs, city government contracted with a private hauler to pick up trash and voted to add the cost plus a little extra revenue for the city's general fund to city utility (water and sewer) bills. Frank Lightle, a community activist who later served with me on the city commission, led a petition drive to force a referendum that outlawed adding the cost to the utility bills without a vote of the people. The referendum won, and city government discontinued picking up the garbage. These cuts in city services were mirrored in most other cities, especially manufacturing cities faced with declining tax bases.

Core Renewal, established when the income tax was increased to 2 percent in 1976, used primarily federal funds to acquire land, demolish old structures, and make the land available for new projects. In time, the downtown Springfield Inn, a new Family YMCA, a large insurance office building, a downtown campus for the local community college, a new library, and a major performing arts center would be built, along with the new city hall. At the same time, streetlights were turned off, trash pickup was discontinued, and other city services deteriorated. Only some of the money could have been spent on the neighborhoods, but residents could not understand how the city could afford all this downtown development while its neighborhoods were visibly deteriorating.

All of this turmoil took its toll on city government itself. Over one five-year period, Springfield had four different city managers. Some city commissioners quit before their terms were completed, and most served only one term. Given the difficulties and stresses of the job, it became increasingly difficult to find people willing to serve on the city commission for just twenty-five hundred dollars a year. There was no light at the end of the tunnel. Springfield fell into a downward cycle in which city government threatened the citizens with some dire consequence if they did not vote for something, the citizens voted no, and then city government imposed the pain. City government bounced from crisis to crisis, employee morale was at rock bottom, and the citizens were mad. By 1989, the city government faced a $1.7 million deficit in its general fund. A new city manager, Matt Kridler, had frozen all new hiring. I asked Frank Lightle, who also was our neighbor and friend, whether I should apply for the vacant seat. He suggested I should do so only if I could handle a lot of heat.

Ironically, I was raised in Silvis, in northwest Illinois, where the farm implement industry went after it left Springfield, Ohio. Most of the boys who graduated with me in 1961 from United Township High School in East Moline went directly to work for John Deere or International Harvester making combines, tractors, corn pickers, and manure spreaders primarily for America's breadbasket. As a child, I rode the bus with my mom to downtown Moline to shop at Sears and Penney's and Woolworth's and the New York Store—just as people did in Springfield, Ohio. Most of the people I grew up among were blue-collar with some poor folks mixed in. My parents did not complete high school because of family difficulties, but unlike most of my fellow graduates from United Township High School, I went off to college. Then came seminary and graduate school. By the time I received my PhD, I had participated briefly in the civil rights movement, been introduced to process theology, joined the campaign of Robert Kennedy in Indiana, written a dissertation on poverty and welfare, and worked for a statewide religious consortium on governmental affairs. However, when we moved to Springfield in 1977 so I could teach at Wittenberg University, it felt like I was back home.

So when I hung up from that phone call from Wes Babian inquiring about whether I would be interested in serving on the Springfield City Commission, I was ready. I had explored some jobs elsewhere, some seriously, but none had worked out for all of us. It seemed likely that I was going to be staying at Wittenberg the rest of my career, but I was restless for a change of pace. Our children Scott and Karen had graduated from high school and were out of the house for now. I knew that Springfield was in real trouble, but I felt it was time that I began acting upon all this knowledge and those principles I had developed. I thought I brought to the task some unusual qualifications. I was well educated but had never cut off my working-class roots. I was committed to social justice but had practiced the capacity to understand and appreciate differences of opinion. I worked at a bastion of Northside Springfield, Wittenberg University, but we had lived and raised our children on the Southside.

ANSWERING THE CALL → to justice, through faith

Clara thought this was a great opportunity and urged me to apply. I applied, was appointed, and sworn in. My adventure in urban politics had begun. For me, this political adventure was also an ethical and religious test. When I came forward to the strains of "Just as I Am" to confess my faith and join First Christian Church as an early teenager, mine was a faith of relationships with family and church. However, I knew that faith led my parents to take responsibility not just for us but for the community. From the beginning, that faith included the least of these as well as the important people. I came to believe that this faith required justice for all as well as love for those I knew. That concept became a principle for action for me through my puny participation in the civil rights movement which taught me to take responsibility for creating greater justice and to believe that my action could make a difference. I brought that religious faith with me when I began my life as an urban politician.

GETTING STARTED

When I joined the Springfield City Commission in 1988, the relationship between the commission and the voters was so toxic that my first job was to establish an identity separate from the sitting commission without irritating the other commissioners so much that they would not work with me. To do that, I chose two issues to oppose: tax abatement and downtown development. If it had not been these two, I would have had to find others. Luckily those issues appealed to the alienated voters, and I thought I was actually right to take the stances I had staked out.

For me, tax abatement was an easy call. In 1988, the practice of Springfield city government was to offer to abate 100 percent of the property taxes for ten years for businesses building new facilities or remodeling or expanding old ones. At that time, the only property taxes the city collected were sent to the state of Ohio for police and firefighter pensions. Most of the city's revenue came from the municipal income tax, which state law did not allow it to abate at that time. While property taxes supported a large number of taxing bodies, by far the largest portion (around 80 percent) went to the public schools. Springfield's practice meant that the schools received no taxes on most construction and new equipment for its first ten years on the tax rolls.

What bothered me most was the effect on schools. I believed, and still believe, that the quality of public education was a key to Springfield's success or failure. Part of the reason people settle in a town is the quality of its schools; the number-one reason they move out of a city is schools. This issue was particularly important in Springfield. The educational level of our population was lower than most comparable cities in Ohio, even the old industrial ones, and we had a high dropout rate. This problem was personal for the individuals with less education, but it was also a major economic problem for our community. Employers who needed an educated workforce, which increasingly means those that pay good wages, might not choose to locate in Springfield or might move to a community with better-educated workers.

The city staff and my fellow commissioners honestly believed that abating these property taxes was in the long-term best interests of everyone, including the schools. Otherwise, the prevailing thinking went, new businesses might well choose to locate somewhere else that offered better tax breaks. Our schools, so people thought, would gain the taxes from these businesses in ten years. In the meantime, there would be spin-off expansion in the tax base as other businesses did business with those receiving the tax breaks and the workers holding the new jobs bought houses. Some truth underlies all of these arguments. The trick in luring new business is to give away as little as possible without losing the prospect, and knowing exactly where that point was is difficult. In this case, I could not help but suspect that it was just too easy for negotiators for the city to give away the school taxes.

I voted against the first tax abatement that came up and lost 4-1. In principle, I oppose all tax abatement. I think businesses should decide on economic grounds where to locate—not on the basis of which community is most willing to hurt its schools. I do not think that the state of Ohio should allow tax abatement, and I think that the federal government should provide significant incentives to all states that do not allow it. I have made this clear to my state and federal representatives more than once, to no avail. Having made my point, I met with staff to create some alternative policy recognizing that other communities would continue to offer abatements. The new policy had two primary features: (1) except in unusual situations, the city would offer to abate no more than 50 percent of the property tax for no more than five years, and (2) the Board of Education would be presented with each deal and allowed to comment upon it. The new policy was adopted and has been city policy since.

This first encounter with legislating said something about politics, but it also represented a fundamental issue facing city governments, especially ones that are not doing very well economically. Because jobs are so important to the health of the community, cities are under pressure to provide incentives (usually including tax breaks) that may attract or keep business, often at the cost of services to citizens. The businesses themselves may need those very services in the long run, in this case an educated workforce. At some point, politics is always the art of the possible. Holding out for pure principles is central to the role of a prophet but threatens to make a politician irrelevant. On the other hand, compromise uninformed by principle is not likely to produce much positive change. Urban politicians constantly must be looking for the proper balance between compromise and principle.

The issue of downtown development was less clear. The 1980s was a time of downward spiral in Springfield, leaving us with no garbage collection, two-thirds of our streetlights turned off, and a visible decline in basic services. In the midst of this crisis, Springfield was proceeding with an ambitious redevelopment of the downtown, including—as mentioned earlier—plans for a new city hall, a new Family YMCA, a new library, a performing arts center, a new bus garage, and a hotel. Some of my colleagues shared my doubts that a downtown hotel could succeed, but they had promised to support it. However, the project would have required federal grant money, money that I felt could have been better spent on the city's neighborhoods. I felt that if it was a good project, it should not have required so much public investment. I decided to vote against spending any more federal grant money on the hotel, explaining that I supported downtown redevelopment and hoped that the Springfield Inn succeeded but that, given the conditions in our neighborhoods, we should not spend the money they needed on the hotel.

In retrospect, I am not sure that I was right about the substance of those votes. The Springfield Inn—now totally remodeled as a Courtyard by Marriott—has been fairly successful as a business and greatly successful as a community meeting place. The total amount of money that could have been spent on the neighborhoods probably would not have made much difference. However, the symbolic politics of these votes was on target. They cast me in the role of the defender of the average people at a time when they felt under siege. Finally, someone was standing up for them. A year later when I was in an election contest with several avowed advocates of putting the neighborhoods first, my credentials already were set in the public's mind. Luckily, I never had a direct showdown with the hotel's supporters. The other four commissioners kept voting yes, and I never criticized the project itself. A few years later as mayor, I helped cut the ribbon at the grand opening of the Springfield Inn. Talk about having your cake and eating it, too.

Again, my experience is common for urban politicians. Downtowns everywhere have suffered from the development of regional and super malls out in the suburbs. Downtowns are never likely to be what they once were, except in a very few cities, but downtowns can either be rallying points for civic pride or symbols of a community's decline. At the same time, the vast majority of cities find it difficult to maintain the quality of basic services to their residential neighborhoods. Downtowns and neighborhoods both need more help than most cities can afford. As I was to learn more and more over time, our choices are seldom clear and almost never without significant trade-offs, what economists call opportunity costs. We often think ethics is simply about choosing between right and wrong. Sometimes it is. More often it is about choosing between the better of two goods or the lesser of two evils. Such choices require judgment and faith, but that is true for all of life, not just urban politics.

STOPPING THE BLEEDING

How is budget cutting an ethical issue? I would argue that it is the most important ethical issue in government. Revenue represents the time and effort of taxpayers taken away from them in order to buy some public goods. Expenditures are a statement about what we hold to be important. Since local governments are not able to run deficits in their operating budgets, a deficit forces hard choices. As we sat around the commissioners' table in 1988 and 1989, our discussion centered upon just how important a particular service was compared to other services. Is a worker in the forestry department more or less important than a police officer? That question is never put to most citizens. They want the tree trimmed in front of their house, and they want police response when they call 911.

So how does a city commissioner decide? One way would be to try to find out what the taxpayers want and do it. That is one approach to democracy; our representatives merely reflect our wishes and thus our values. As we convened around that budget table in 1989, any or all of us may at times have taken the popularity of services into account. However, we also believed that we were elected by the people to make the hard decisions and that we had access to a lot more information than the average citizen. Our primary concern was what we thought were the most important services. We hated to eliminate foresters, but we believed police protection was more important. The bases upon which you and I decide what is most important are our ethical principles, and they finally are grounded in our most fundamental life commitments: our faith. For me, I tried to protect programs that met basic needs or primarily served people with fewer resources. A program that served primarily affluent people was suspect in my mind. The trouble was that there was not much luxury in the Springfield budget that had not already been cut out by 1988. It also did not do any good to cut a program that was either essentially free, because it broke even, or that produced income even though it was a relative luxury, such as our golf courses. Most cities for at least the past twenty years have been faced with budget cutting. While these budget decisions receive little media attention, they are the most fundamental choices city governments make.

One step in the downward spiral of the Springfield of the 1980s was the turning off of two-thirds of the streetlights. The lights on major streets and near intersections were left on, but the rest were turned off to save electricity. Streetlights are not as important as some other matters, but lights that are dark are very visible. The dark lights took on symbolic significance far beyond their real importance, the most obvious indication that Springfield was a failure. How could city government convince citizens it could do anything else if it could not even turn the lights on again? So Matt Kridler, the city manager, approached our local utility, Ohio Edison, with a problem. We needed to turn our streetlights back on, but we had very little money. Matt argued that turning on the streetlights in Springfield would stimulate economic development and thus increase business for the utility over time. The result was an agreement that was not perfect, but it was a pretty good deal. We doubted that citizens cared about the specifics as long as the lights were lit. The deal was approved, and Ohio Edison began to reconnect our lights.

By election day of 1989, I had established myself as an independent voice on the city commission, the new city manager had stopped the bleeding in the city budget, and the streetlights were about to shine again. That made it a good time for me to run. But a revolution was brewing.

THE REVOLUTION

Adopted in 1913, the charter of the city of Springfield established the city manager form of government and called for the election to four-year terms of five city commissioners running citywide without party label. This was intended to keep politics out of city government. As far as I know, at no time since the adoption of that charter had there been more than one Democrat or more than one person who lived on the Southside of Springfield on the city commission. Over that time, the Eastside and Westside were represented even less than the Southside. Republicans from the Northside, the more affluent part of Springfield, ran city government for seventy-five years. By the 1980s, there was broad support for the need to assure that all parts of the city were represented on the commission. However, an attempt to revise the charter to establish wards also included a major increase in compensation for city commissioners, so it failed.

The election was close, but in the end I was elected to the commission with the most votes and named mayor by my fellow commissioners. I had a good team with me on the commission, including two other Democrats who lived within blocks of each other on the Southside of town. What we three shared was a commitment to improving the lives of average people in the blue-collar and low-income neighborhoods of Springfield. From the outside, this was either a breath of fresh air that brought new hope or a scary new world of uncertainty. All agreed that it promised to be different.

I arrived early for the swearing-in ceremony on January 2, 1990, wearing the last suit my dad bought before he died. The City Hall Forum was soon full, mostly of family and supporters of the three new commissioners. I could not help but think how proud my parents would have been to have been there. The hour before the actual meeting was filled with music—classical music from a Wittenberg group; bluegrass from four women, including a mother of one of Clara's former students; and a gospel group from Dale Henry's church. They sang our desire to be the city commission of all of Springfield's people. A new day had begun for the city. As I stood with Clara, my hand upraised to repeat the oaths given by a municipal court judge, reality began to hit home. In a little over one year I had gone from a somewhat bored college professor looking for something worth doing to a college professor who was also the mayor of a struggling old industrial city. Now I certainly had enough to do, and I was convinced it was worth doing. Almost as soon as we were sworn in we needed to replace outgoing mayor Tim Ayers, who decided to move to Columbus. We quickly appointed Nora Parker to that seat.

The new commission was an interesting group. The only Republican and Northsider on the council was Faye Flack. The other four of us all were Democrats who lived on the Southside, but what a delightful mix. Faye supported business interests but was committed to equal rights. Frank Lightle was the hero of the Appalachian community. Dale Henry had good contacts in the African American community. Nora Parker was a government teacher at South High School and a longtime political activist for the Springfield Education Association. And then there was me, with one foot in Wittenberg and one in our Southside neighborhood. All five of us were connected to different constituencies, but all were committed to bridging the antagonism between city government and the citizens.

All cities have the problem of whether their elected body represents the entire community and especially whether it represents those parts of the community not usually represented. Often this concern is seen as a trade-off with having an elected body that is able to see the big picture instead of the particular concerns of the special constituencies. This problem affects all elected bodies, but cities are often seen as either dominated by a narrow elite or torn apart by parochial interests. The tension is real. People, especially disadvantaged groups, need to be represented, but the common interest also needs to be represented. This commission met both of these needs quite well for Springfield.

SYMBOLIC CHANGES

Rightly or wrongly, many citizens of Springfield believed that a lot of deals involving city government in 1990 were made behind closed doors. Ohio had an Open Meetings Act that allowed a majority of us to meet in private only for certain purposes, such as personnel, pending litigation, property purchases and sales, or labor negotiations. In Ohio, statutory cities are ruled by the state laws on municipalities, while a charter city has its own local constitution that it follows unless it contradicts state or federal laws. Springfield is a charter city, giving us more freedom in how we operate, so we did not have to follow the Open Meetings Act. However, the new commission decided that it would be a good symbol of our openness to the public if we asked the voters to include the provisions of the state's Open Meeting Act in the charter of the city of Springfield. We voted to put that on the ballot for May 1990, and it passed. This move was mostly symbolic, but symbols can be powerful.

At the same time, Springfield was wrestling with the underlying issues of jobs, tax base, and basic services that are fundamental to city government. I always felt that the symbolic issues were less significant. Yet the media picked up on the symbolic and generally ignored or gave just passing attention to the fundamentals. Television cameras appeared for discussions of curfews or gun control but never showed up for budget adoption. Part of it was complexity. The city budget was big and complicated. A city commissioner or a reporter had to spend a lot of time and ask a lot of questions to understand it. Only the newspaper reporter tried; the radio and television people could not spend the time it took. Part of it was attention span. Retaining jobs and bringing new ones to town would provide a lot more jobs than some short-term city jobs program, but this approach took time. The broadcast media did not have the time to wait. Perhaps the citizens themselves also could not or would not take the time to understand the complicated or wait for results.

I reluctantly reached the conclusion that while I must stay focused on fundamentals, I also needed to learn to play some symbolic politics. I do not think that any of the symbolic moves we made to communicate openness stood in the way of important business. People did seem to think we were more open, and the changes had not really caused any big problems. I had stumbled into what became a principle for me. If a symbolic act did not do any significant harm and seemed to respond to something people cared about, why not do it? It might give people a false sense that we were doing something about a problem when we were not, but even that might be at least therapeutic.

I believe that the changes we made in commission procedures did not really change much except the public's perception of us. However, that perception had to be changed for us to be able to move ahead with real problems. I guess I was becoming more political, but I made a mental note to myself to remember what was really important. I did not ever want to delude myself into thinking I was really doing much by passing legislation that was only symbolic. Urban politicians face this temptation since they are short on money and because the media, especially broadcast media, are focused on symbols. Symbols work in the short run, but reality tends to catch up over time with merely symbolic gestures.

FUNDAMENTAL REALITIES

All of us elected in 1989 had run on the basis of returning basic services to the community. Newly relit streetlights were a start, but safety and jobs were much more fundamental. When I was named to the city commission in September 1988, the city was in the midst of a campaign to pass a property tax levy that would have provided operating funds for the city, including the safety forces. After a couple of failures, a group of citizens was able to pass a levy to increase the number of police on the street. This move allowed us not only to put more officers on the beat but also to initiate community-oriented policing aimed at putting the police in better contact with the people in our neighborhoods.

The local economy is central to everything a city tries to do. The transition away from heavy manufacturing by well-paid union workers that is centered in the Midwest and especially in Ohio already was under way in Springfield in 1988. It has accelerated since. In 1988, employment at the then–Navistar International was sixty-five hundred; the now–International Truck and Engine employs fewer than one thousand workers in Springfield. The jobs lost extend beyond International to its suppliers and to those people who sell goods and services to the International workers. This situation has forced a psychic shift from a solid blue-collar town to a town that has lost the center of its economy—leaving those at the top and those at the bottom, but a lot fewer in the middle.

The truth is that the primary driver of local employment was the strength of the national economy. When the national economy grows, businesses expand— some of them in Ohio and some in Springfield. Like all cities, we try to get more than our share. When the national economy contracts, local jobs are lost. Like all cities, we try to lose less than our share. Actually, Springfield held its own in Ohio in terms of the number of jobs. The trouble was that most of the new jobs did not pay as well as the ones that were lost. In our competitive economy and federal system, cities are forced to compete with other cities for jobs. This competition is not always fair and may undercut other important priorities, as we saw earlier in terms of tax abatements.

CHANGES

Over the years there were many changes to the city commission. While the Southside majority survived throughout these changes, I did not survive as mayor. In both 1994 and 1996, the commission tore itself apart over who should hold that post. I continued on the city commission, but both times others were elected mayor. These were difficult years for a number of reasons, but I tried to be a good loser. Between 1994 and 1998, my primary way of being a good loser was to shift the extra time I had given to being mayor into my own professional life. One result was a book, *And the Poor Get Welfare*,[7] that picked up on my dissertation work, updated it, and related it to President Bill Clinton's welfare reform proposals. The other result was the collaboration with David Rusk that resulted in Updating the Dream.

CITIES AS A MORAL ISSUE

So there you have the story of how I became an urban politician. Along the way in the story I have pointed out the extent to which the realities of Springfield are very typical of cities generally and especially of industrial cities and particularly those in the Midwest and Northeast regions of the United States. I have also identified a series of challenges such cities face these days. Fiscally, cities have less revenue and greater demand for services and must deal with the trade-off between preserving those basic services and attracting and keeping jobs and downtown redevelopment. Urban politicians must constantly struggle with how much time to spend with primarily symbolic efforts instead of trying to address fundamental problems. Most basically, cities must deal with the loss of manufacturing jobs, the drain caused by sprawl to the suburbs, and the serious divisions of race and income among their citizens.

The thesis of this book is that these are not just practical problems but taken together pose a fundamental issue of justice in our society. Our metropolitan areas are increasingly sorting out into neighborhoods that are homogeneous by race and income. Put directly, the way our metropolitan areas are organized is destroying the lives of far too many of our people, imposing dramatically different costs on different groups of our citizens and failing to provide communities that bring us together as people. I firmly believe that we will have great difficulty facing this injustice without coming to terms with our most fundamental commitments. This is finally a matter of faith. We shall return to this consideration of ethics, justice, and faith, but first we need to understand better the practical, unjust situation in which cities find themselves. In Springfield we did that through the process we called *Updating the Dream*.

Chapter 2

Rusk's Elasticity Stretches Springfield

By 1994, things actually were getting better in Springfield, largely because the local economy had improved along with the national economy, even if it lagged a step or two behind. The city budget was coming into balance, and services were being restored. City government had carried out a full review of city services and how we delivered them, producing a strategic plan for the future. As a result, our city manager, Matt Kridler, was named the Miami Valley Public Manager of the Year for 1995. Kathy Kridler was a good sounding board for her husband. One day in 1996, she told him that she had heard a fellow named David Rusk on public radio who seemed to be saying many of the things Matt had talked about with her. Matt ordered Rusk's book, *Cities without Suburbs*,[1] read it, and shared it with me. When I checked with Wittenberg's urban studies faculty, Rob Baker, our urban political scientist, knew Rusk's work and admired it. Matt and I agreed that we should contact Rusk. It turned out that he was coming to Dayton for a regional conference. Matt arranged for Rusk to have breakfast with him and all of the available commissioners while Rusk was in Dayton.

My first reaction was that he looked a lot like his father, Dean Rusk, secretary of state during the Vietnam War. My second reaction was that he spoke clearly, made sense, and already had learned a lot about Springfield from basic census data. We decided to pursue a working arrangement with Rusk to do an analysis of Springfield, and a month or so later, he came to the city. In a meeting with Matt and me, he presented a written analysis of another community as a model of what might be shared with ours before he came to town. I suggested that the Wittenberg Urban Studies Program faculty could do the study and that Wittenberg could include Rusk in its lecture series.

I was the director of urban studies at Wittenberg. We were a small program, offering only a minor in a liberal arts college. When I asked the urban studies faculty if they would be interested in a project like the one Rusk had done for the other community, some were enthusiastic, and all were willing. Wittenberg president Baird Tipson was very interested in the college helping bring Rusk to town. A plan emerged. The Wittenberg urban studies team would produce an analysis of Springfield that would be made public, David Rusk would speak on how Springfield compared to other communities with which he had worked and would make recommendations for our future, and the community would meet to discuss how to proceed. Being college professors, the Wittenberg team imagined a published collection of essays and went about producing the essays. Finding no one to finance the publication of the essays and doubting that such a publication would be read broadly, Matt and I decided to try for a shorter insert in the Sunday newspaper as Rusk had done in York, Pennsylvania. My job was to get the team to produce the larger volume and to condense that larger work into twenty pages for the average citizen of Springfield.

On Sunday, March 30, 1997, a twenty-page newspaper insert titled "Updating the Dream: Springfield Looks at 2000 and Beyond" appeared in the *Springfield News-Sun*.[2] It was a summary of the research done by the Wittenberg Urban Studies Program but soon became known locally as the Rusk Report. I wrote the insert and edited and wrote about half of the larger volume of over a hundred pages, duplicated by the city of Springfield print shop. The newspaper insert contained pictures and maps; the larger volume had more charts and footnotes. We still use the larger study in our urban studies courses at Wittenberg, but the insert was a good means of presenting the information to the public. That week David Rusk spoke to a large audience, including a good number of townspeople, at Wittenberg. During the morning of the following day, the public had an opportunity to discuss Rusk's suggestions at greater length, and he responded to that discussion after lunch. On the basis of that discussion, local task groups were set up to pursue the recommendations and propose specific local action.

Rusk began his speech by discussing Springfield and Clark County and how we fit into his analysis of other cities. As expected, he found us typical in most ways. He gave us great credit for the determination with which we had responded to significant job losses, calling Springfield "the comeback kid." He then made his case for the importance of a vital core community in any metropolitan area, meaning a strong Springfield in Clark County. He argued that the signature community sets the tone for its surrounding area. Finally, he made a pitch for cooperation between cities and the surrounding areas, insisting that cities cannot solve their problems without solutions that include the entire metropolitan area. He said that since Ohio made metropolitan government so difficult to create, this must be done through other means of cooperation. He made clear that these means would continue to include annexation. Using data from the Wittenberg study, Rusk pointed out the problems created by concentrating poor people in certain neighborhoods and showed pictures of the dispersal of low- and moderate-income housing in Montgomery County, Maryland. Developers there are required to include a portion of moderate- and low-income housing in middle- and upper-income housing developments. This strategy helps spread poverty out instead of concentrating it in poor, inner-city neighborhoods. His entire presentation was a specific application of his general ideas to Springfield.

RUSK'S RECOMMENDATIONS

Rusk then offered three specific suggestions for future action in Springfield and Clark County. First was what he called win-win annexation. The practice at that time was to withdraw land from its township when it was annexed to Springfield. Instead, he suggested that the property be left in its township and that Springfield share some of its income tax with the township. In this way, the city and the townships would win from annexation. Second was comprehensive land-use planning. He urged the city and the county to establish a joint comprehensive land-use plan that laid out where development of various sorts should occur and then have the courage to use it to make decisions. Third was a housing dispersal program. He advocated a program for Ohio similar to Montgomery County, Maryland. Given the nature of Ohio state law and the dispersal of our housing, he did not believe it was possible to accomplish this objective simply on a county basis. Thus, he proposed state legislation for this purpose. The discussion on the second day was generally supportive of these three proposals, and the study groups that were set up recommended that local officials pursue all three.

So what was David Rusk's analysis that we brought to bear on Springfield? We focused on two big ideas: elasticity and concentration of poverty. Elasticity is the basic insight that inspired Rusk's *Cities without Suburbs*,[3] establishing him as a major new voice in our thinking about cities. The concentration-of-poverty concept first was introduced clearly by William Julius Wilson in *The Truly Disadvantaged*,[4] a book that established him as the most influential urban sociologist of our time. The descriptions of these two concepts that follow are shaped by those two books.

ELASTICITY

David Rusk begins his discussion of elasticity[5] by recognizing that the vast majority of urban growth around the country is occurring at the periphery—the outer edges of the cities. He shows that this is true of all American cities, regardless of location and in spite of what local officials may do to revitalize downtowns or rehabilitate older neighborhoods. Scattered successes at saving the old do not change the dominant trends. Most developers of housing, shopping, and even industry want to locate on previously undeveloped land at the edge of cities. Given this basic push to development at the outer edge, Rusk defines an elastic city as one that captures this growth (including it within the city) and an inelastic city as one that allows the growth to escape (losing it to the surrounding area). Elastic cities retain the tax base essential to the continued funding of city services; inelastic cities lose their tax base to the surrounding area and find it increasingly difficult to fund city services.

In Ohio, Columbus is an elastic city. Using utilities as an incentive, Columbus pushed its boundaries out into then-undeveloped areas in the 1950s. Thus, in the years since, Columbus has been able to include most new growth in its metropolitan area within the city limits. This approach—plus state government, the state university, and a lot of other growing service industries—has made Columbus the go-go city of Ohio. Cleveland and, even closer to us, Dayton are inelastic cities. Dayton is nearly surrounded by suburbs. Interstate 675 has created around the city a growth corridor where the vast majority of new development is occurring. Suburbs like Centerville, Beavercreek, and Fairborn are the boom cities in the Dayton metropolitan area. In spite of dramatic efforts by its leadership, Dayton has begun the decline that Cleveland has experienced for decades.

According to Rusk, elastic cities are much more able to provide and finance higher-quality public services within their metropolitan areas. Schools are better, and crime is lower. Elastic cities experience less racial and economic segregation. He thinks that many suburbs set up hurdles intended to keep the poor and nonwhite population to a minimum. Elastic cities as a group experience greater economic development for the entire metropolitan areas of which they are a part. The Columbus region is better off with a healthy, growing Columbus at its center. At a minimum, political boundaries make it harder for people and their leaders to think of a metropolitan area as a whole. On the other hand, Rusk argues that inelastic cities tend to be cities in trouble. Inelastic cities do not remain constant; they decline. As they lose tax base, these cities are less able to finance quality public services. Schools deteriorate, and crime increases. Racial and economic segregation increases as whites and those with more resources move to the suburbs. The metropolitan areas around inelastic cities experience less economic development. Rusk argues that the entire Dayton and Cleveland areas are worse off with inelastic, declining cities at their cores. At a minimum, people and their leaders are almost forced to think of a metropolitan area as a whole if it is one political unit. The Wittenberg urban studies team set out to examine whether Springfield was elastic or inelastic. In *Cities without Suburbs*, Rusk had placed Springfield in his low-elasticity category.[6] If Rusk was right about that and about the consequences that flow from that reality, Springfield and the entire surrounding region were in trouble.

ELASTICITY IN SPRINGFIELD

Before we turned to the issue of elasticity, we identified three basic characteristics of Springfield and Clark County.[7] First, although Dayton television and radio stations claim they serve the Dayton-Springfield area and the Bureau of the Census places the cities together in the same MSA (Metropolitan Statistical Area), Springfield is not a suburb of Dayton or Columbus. Perhaps the simplest test of economic connection is where we work. The vast majority of workers in Springfield and in the suburban townships around Springfield work in Springfield or elsewhere in Clark County. With the exception of some areas in the western end of Clark County that orient more to suburban Dayton, residents of Springfield and Clark County depend upon this area as their primary economic base.

Second, Springfield often is described as an old Midwest industrial city, and so it is in many ways. International Truck and Engine has been the largest employer and the payer of the best manufacturing wages for decades. Other industrial firms, paying various levels of wages, are located around the community. However, the manufacturing sector has declined over the recent decades while wholesale and retail trade and service employment rose. One way of expressing this transition is to compare the top-ten Springfield employers in 1950 with the top ten in 2000. In 1950, nine of the top-ten payrolls were manufacturers; Springfield truly was a factory town very typical of America's industrial heartland of that day. By 2005, the ten largest firms in the city, as measured by the size of their income tax withholding accounts, tell a different story. We find only one manufacturer (Honda, not International), one call center, and one restaurant supply company, along with four providers of services (including two hospitals), and three governmental employers. The manufacturing sector remains important to Springfield and Clark County, but less so than in the past. Since agriculture also is important to Clark County, the economy in Springfield and Clark County is much more diverse than it used to be or may appear to be now. This is one case where increasing diversity clearly is a strength, since it makes us less dependent on any single sector of the economy.

Third, when we compared Springfield to other Ohio cities, we found that it is just about as typical as *Newsweek* and the rest of the media have said. It is simplest to say that in almost all ways we fall about midway between Columbus and Cleveland. We compared on a number of measures the census data for Springfield to the three largest cities (Cleveland, Columbus, and Cincinnati), our nearest city (Dayton), and some other Ohio cities of comparable size (Lima, Canton, Lorain, Middletown, and Mansfield). While Springfield fell in the middle of these cities in median family income, a low cost of living increases our buying power. At the time, we measured better on our unemployment rate, which trailed only Columbus, Cincinnati, and Middletown. By 2000, it had inched up a bit in comparison with other Ohio cities. Education and income are tied together so closely today that it is helpful to look at educational attainment and poverty levels at the same time. Springfield had proportionately more high

Table 2.1. Springfield Demographics Compared to Those of Other Ohio Cities

City	Median Family Income 1990	Median Family Income 2000	Unemployment Rate 1990	Unemployment Rate 2000	% not high school graduates 1990	% not high school graduates 2000	% graduated college 1990	% graduated college 2000	% Poverty 1990	% Poverty 2000
Cleveland	$22,448	$30,286	14.0	3.8	41.2	31.0	8.1	11.4	28.7	26.3
Dayton	$24,819	$34,978	10.5	3.9	31.7	24.9	12.3	14.4	26.5	23.0
Canton	$25,177	$35,680	11.3	4.1	33.0	24.9	9.7	11.8	21.9	19.2
Lima	$25,775	$32,405	12.8	4.4	30.7	24.3	8.4	9.5	21.6	22.7
Cincinnati	$26,774	$37,543	7.9	3.6	30.4	24.3	22.2	26.6	24.3	21.9
Springfield	$26,838	$39,890	8.8	4.3	31.7	23.4	10.9	12.7	20.9	16.9
Mansfield	$28,504	$37,541	8.8	5.1	30.3	22.3	13.0	13.4	17.8	16.3
Lorain	$29,304	$39,454	9.3	N/A	32.5	25.7	7.7	9.9	19.8	17.1
Middletown	$31,313	$43,876	7.8	N/A	28.6	24.1	12.8	13.1	15.4	12.6
Columbus	$32,898	$47,391	5.9	3.2	21.3	16.2	24.6	29.0	17.2	14.8

Table 2.2. City Growth in Territory, 1950–1990

Metro Area	City Area in Square Miles (1950)	City Area in Square Miles (1990)	City Area Growth, 1950–1990 (%)	Rusk's City Elasticity Category
Ohio Average	33	56	72	Low
North Carolina Average	14	66	366	High
Springfield	12	20	61	Low
Dayton	25	55	120	Low
Cleveland	75	77	3	Zero
Columbus	39	191	385	High

school dropouts and fewer college graduates than most of these other Ohio cities. This lack of an educated labor force is a problem for attracting and keeping good jobs here, which will be increasingly true in the future, when wages will be tied to education even more closely. Springfield actually had a lower level of poverty than this relatively low educational attainment would predict. This was not a good omen in an economy increasingly rewarding education in employment and wages.

When we turned to the matter of elasticity itself, things become a bit complicated. In order to measure the elasticity of different cities, Rusk created an index of elasticity, which basically measured the territory added to a city in relation to the change in the size of its population. Rusk concluded that Springfield had low elasticity because its boundaries did not expand very much between 1950 and 1990. The average annual rate of growth of Springfield's boundaries for the period 1950–1990 was around 1.5 percent, a relatively low figure, even for Ohio cities. By comparison, Cleveland grew almost not at all during those forty years, while Columbus grew at a rate like a typical North Carolina city. This is one of the few areas where Dayton's numbers look better than Springfield's, but most of its growth was early in the period, and it has very few remaining options for future expansion. Table 2.2 summarizes this information.

Rusk concluded that Ohio's urban areas have experienced low rates of population growth and high rates of land development outside their boundaries. His primary concern is that Ohio's central cities steadily are being abandoned. To raise its elasticity rating to a level comparable to that of Columbus, Springfield would need to be a city three to four times its size in square miles. Had such growth occurred, Springfield would have been categorized as a medium-elasticity city. To reach the high-elasticity category, Springfield would have needed to be seven to eight times its size.

If sprawl and failure to capture growth on the periphery is the problem, annexation can be seen as one solution, according to Rusk. Annexation is the process by which land is brought into a city, extending the city's boundaries. Since 1985, Springfield has pursued what locally has been considered an aggressive annexation policy. Actually, it has stressed annexation of commercial, industrial, and new residential property while offering to provide utilities to established residential areas within utility service districts without annexation. Since the city's primary source of revenue is a tax on wages and profits earned within the city, this approach makes a lot of sense. One way to describe this policy is that the city has sought to annex jobs more than population. Since the city is the only source of public water and sewer service in its surrounding area, very little industrial or commercial development could occur near Springfield without annexation. Already existing utility service districts were in residential areas, the most significant being the Northridge Water and Sewer Districts, located where the Clark County housing boom was centered. As a result, much of the new residential building occurred outside of the city limits with city utilities without annexation under these already existing agreements.

Springfield's most visible annexation efforts in the 1980s and early 1990s were the PrimeOhio industrial park and the North Bechtle commercial area. Located across Ohio Route 41 from the Clark County Fairgrounds, PrimeOhio provided excellent industrial sites with instant access to Interstate 70. Some of these new firms already were present locally, but most had come from outside the area. In either case, they probably would have been lost to Springfield's tax rolls except for the annexation of PrimeOhio. Already by 1996, the added revenue for the North Bechtle development (Wal-Mart, Lowe's, Big Bear, etc.) was estimated at $150,000. When all other annexations are added in, the city estimated that a total of $1 million was added to Springfield's 1996 revenue. By 2005, that figure reached around $3 million in additional annual revenue. These estimates did not include any multiplier effect. That is, they did not include other jobs that either directly or indirectly support those jobs created in the annexed areas. Annexation of the tax base had been key to the economic revival of Springfield city government even if annexation of territory and population has been slow.

FILTERING SPRINGFIELD'S HOUSING

Elasticity is not simply a matter of population and jobs and tax base; it also affects housing. When people move out of a city, they begin a process experts call filtering.[8] A family moves into a new home. They sell their old home to another family, that family sells its home to a third family, and so forth. Often this buying and selling occurs seven or eight times. If this process works well, each family ends up in a somewhat better home. Usually, at each step of the filtering process the price is lower. Often this is reflected in the incomes of the buyers. The first buyer might be quite well off, the next somewhat less well off, the third less well off than the second, and so forth. Somewhere along the line, the transaction also usually changes from home owning to renting. For instance, in a seven-step filtering, the first four families each might be buying a relatively better home or apartment, but the last three might each be renting a relatively better home or apartment. The last step usually involves a rental unit in a low-income neighborhood that now becomes vacant. The property might be rehabilitated, at which point it would begin a new filtering chain. The property might alternatively be boarded up, at which point it becomes a problem for its neighborhood and ultimately for city government.

Economic stagnation in the 1980s in the Midwest, and particularly in Ohio, had been reflected in relatively little construction of new housing. That situation had changed in the years just prior to our study and in the years since because of lower interest rates. In Clark County, this increase in housing production since 1990 had resulted in the construction of a total of 2,352 new housing units between 1990 and 2005. Especially notable had been expensive subdivisions that have sprung up, mostly on the outskirts of town. All of this housing construction had occurred while the population of Clark County was relatively constant. New households, created when children moved out and such, had accounted for only about one-fifth of the housing added to Clark County's supply. The rest had not been needed simply to meet the demand for shelter. This oversupply of housing had resulted in lower prices for existing housing and in vacant structures.

Determining the relative value of housing within Clark County was not easy. Generally, prices for everything tend to go up over time due to inflation. They did for housing in Springfield and Clark County, too. The median house value is the value of the middle house, the house that has just as many houses worth more than it as it has houses worth less than it. The median value of houses in Springfield and Clark County more than tripled between 1970 and 1990. However, when these numbers are adjusted for inflation, the Clark County median house value was exactly the same in 1990 as in 1970, and the Springfield median house value actually declined by more than 12 percent. Over the same period, the inflation-adjusted median value of housing in the United States went up more than 36 percent, and the inflation-adjusted median housing value for Ohio went up almost 7 percent. In sum, housing was relatively inexpensive in Springfield and Clark County. Positively, the result is that we can afford better housing than in other cities, which is one big reason that the cost of living in Springfield and Clark County is relatively low. We live better here than our same incomes would buy in many other places in the United States. Negatively, our houses bring a lower sales price if we decide to sell them.

This data still did not tell us just what effect new housing had on the value of our older houses. One way to do this was to figure out how much the houses in one neighborhood (say, a census tract) were worth compared to the average for the county in 1970. Then we could figure out the same thing for 1990. This would tell us if the houses in that neighborhood had increased or decreased in value compared to the rest of the Clark County. We could use census data that was pretty dependable and covered every house in the area for the comparison of 1970 to 2000. Table 2.3 details what happened to the relative value of housing in Clark County. For instance, housing values in census tract 3 (Selma Road) declined 29 percent in relative value, compared to the county as a whole over these two decades. The central and southern city tracts declined in relative value, with those neighborhoods with lower relative value in 1970 usually experiencing the greatest decline. The last step in the filtering process usually was in low-income neighborhoods, leaving vacant structures and low property values. This came as absolutely no surprise and is true of inner-city neighborhoods across the United States.

The real news was that housing values in Northside neighborhoods did better but also declined in comparison to county values. Unlike most cities, traditionally the most expensive housing in Springfield had been inside the city. Springfield had not had any exclusive suburbs with predominantly affluent residents. The residents of its suburbs had been mostly middle-income people, many of them workers in manufacturing. In 1970, the Ridgewood tracts (18 and 19) that long had been considered the prime places to live in the entire county had the highest relative value in the county. By 1990, however, all the suburban tracts listed here—except the southern (older) part of Northridge—had passed Ridgewood in median housing value. Census tracts are divided into smaller units called blocks. An examination of block data showed that some suburban neighborhoods also were declining. An example was the two neighborhoods in the older part of Northridge, which was the largest suburban development outside the city where many of the International workers lived. In each case, the mean value of their housing had dropped more than 10 percent between 1970 and 1990. While this decline was less than for many city neighborhoods, it nevertheless was headed in the same direction. The conclusion seemed clear: building a lot of new housing in an area with little population growth caused the value of already-existing housing to decline. The decline seemed to be greatest in the older low-income neighborhoods, but more affluent neighborhoods of older housing were not immune from similar, if less dramatic, results. Some of the winners of the past are now becoming losers. Today's winners may be vulnerable to similar declining values in the future.

The 2000 data showed some interesting changes.[9] The lowest-income census tracts actually experienced some increase in relative values. Since they also experienced a significant decline in housing units, this improvement probably resulted from demolishing a significant number of the lowest-value homes. Housing values in the middle-income neighborhoods continued to decline, but at a slower rate. The highest-income city tract experienced an increased rate of decline in relative value. The older suburban tracts also saw significant decline in relative housing values between 1990 and 2000. The overall lesson is that former winners in and out of the city are now beginning to see the kind of decline in relative housing values that older urban neighborhoods saw in the past.

Filtering produces much more visible results in our older neighborhoods. One result is the decline of home ownership in many city neighborhoods. Most experts believe that people who own their homes tend to take better care of

Table 2.3. Census Tract Median House Value Compared to the County Median Housing Value

Census Tract Number	Neighborhood Name	1970 Ratio	1990 Ratio	Change 1970–1990	2000 Ratio	Change 1990–2000
3	Selma Road	0.51	0.36	−29%	0.41	+14%
9.02	South Yellow Springs	0.67	0.55	−18%	0.59	+7%
11.02	Southgate	1.04	0.74	−29%	0.71	−4%
13	Kenwood Heights	0.88	0.74	−16%	0.72	−3%
18	Ridgewood	1.33	1.21	−9%	1.07	−12%
20	Forest Hills	1.27	1.32	+4%	1.28	−3%
22	Shawnee	1.21	1.32	+9%	1.32	0
25	German Township	1.28	1.26	−2%	1.31	+4%
23.02	Northridge (N)	1.21	1.30	+7%	1.16	−11%
24.01	Northridge (S)	1.23	1.20	−2%	1.12	−7%

them. Homeowners also seem to get more involved in efforts at neighborhood preservation or revitalization. Outside of the city, the number of owner-occupied housing units went up 16.3 percent between 1970 and 1990. Inside the city, they went down 0.7 percent during the same time. However, the amount of home ownership varies dramatically from one part of town to another. The central, southwestern, southeastern, and eastern parts of Springfield all experienced significant (−7.7 percent to −12.9 percent) declines in home ownership. Over the same period, home ownership in the north of town went up 20.8 percent. A significant and growing issue in Springfield is foreclosures; as expected, they are much more common in low-income neighborhoods. At the end of the filtering process, after everyone has moved up, is usually a rental unit so bad that no one wants to live in it. Because of the age of much of our housing, we have many such units in Springfield, which is probably why the homeless population is as small as it is. Nearly every household can find an apartment cheap enough that they can manage the rent. However, the unit may well be dilapidated.

If no one wants to rent the apartment or city inspectors find it in violation of the housing code, the structure has to be secured so that strangers cannot enter it, which typically involves putting plywood over the windows. As long as access at ground level has been closed off and the building is structurally sound, further action to force rehabilitation is difficult. These boarded-up structures are major concerns for neighbors. Often, although they are boarded up, they really are not secured. Persons may break in to live in them even without heat and utilities. Young people may use them as hangouts, and the units could be the site of illegal activity. In any event, they are clear, visible signs of neighborhood deterioration.

One solution is to rehabilitate them so that they can be rented again or sold to homeowners. However, the trends in housing values make that very difficult. Full rehabilitation often is almost as expensive as building new. One factor that determined the value of a house is the neighborhood in which it was located. Many of Springfield's neighborhoods have very low median housing values that continue to decline. Given construction costs, it is impossible to bring vacant structures up to the housing code without investing much more than the value at which the house will be appraised. This reality makes private investors reluctant to invest in such housing rehabilitation without significant government subsidies. However, that money is drying up. Besides, federal requirements that housing rehabilitated with government money must be totally brought up to the building code drive rehabilitation costs much higher than the private market will spend on its own. As a result, there is nearly no significant rehabilitation of housing in our low-income neighborhoods by the private market. What rehabilitation is done is limited in amount and largely subsidized with federal housing funds.

One final solution is demolition. Springfield orders many owners to demolish property that has deteriorated so far that rehabilitation is very costly. The city also has greatly increased the amount of demolition in recent years. In 1990, when this increased demolition began, a drive-by survey of vacant structures found 225 such properties. In 1995, after all of this demolition, a similar survey found 458; in a more systematic study done in 2001, the number remained about 500. While about 100 residential structures are demolished each year, new vacant structures are being created as quickly as they can be rehabilitated or demolished. This was one very visible way in which building new housing led to problems for the low-income neighborhoods at the end of the filtering process. The low interest rates that led to a building boom in suburban areas helped create lower housing values in almost all city neighborhoods and boarded-up structures in our low-income neighborhoods.

POLITICAL FRAGMENTATION: SUBURBS

One last part of Rusk's analysis that we looked at was the extent to which local government was fragmented,[10] making a metropolitan view of issues and concerted action on them difficult. The underlying tension between the urban center and the suburban fringe that permeated the findings of the study also was present in the political system in Clark County. There was a time when suburbs were either small towns or urban areas not very different from the central city but with a different government. Even the word "suburb" itself has taken on a different connotation over the years. Earlier, the term implied a relationship to a particular city, whereas today it implies being distinct from the city. This is evident, for example, when one simply compares the names of older suburbs such as South Chicago or East St. Louis with those of newer suburbs like Forest Hills and Florissant. By 1990, a majority of Americans reported that they lived in suburbs. Increasingly, people move to the suburbs to get away from the problems of the city. One principal source of political conflict over the last several years has been the national trend toward segregation along class and racial lines supported by the fragmentation of political authority in metropolitan areas. A primary function of most suburban governments has become keeping urban problems out of their communities. The upshot has been that those living on the periphery are less and less concerned with the problems of the central cities that they have left behind.

In the latter part of the nineteenth century, central cities were able to recapture through aggressive annexation the resources represented by the fringe developments. But as the twentieth century moved on and suburban areas gained greater representation in state legislatures, many states adopted restrictive annexation laws, making it almost impossible for most central cities to employ this strategy further. Nationally, this approach usually produced tension between cities and suburbs that had themselves become incorporated as cities. Certainly this was typical of Ohio cities, but it is not true of Springfield. Springfield has no suburbs that are themselves cities; we are surrounded by suburban areas in townships. This fact is important because townships in Ohio do not have many of the powers that incorporated cities have. People living in Springfield's suburban areas may well share the antiurban attitudes of suburbanites across the country, but they just do not have as much capacity under the law to act upon those attitudes.

One aspect of political fragmentation in metropolitan areas is the growing polarization of the attitudes of central-city residents and suburban residents about what to do about metropolitan problems. Suburban governments, largely townships in our case, exercise considerable control over what happens in their area and are reluctant to give that up, especially to city governments. This is reinforced by the view that cities have problems with which suburbs simply do not want to deal. Different locations produce different perceived interests. In a study of residents of the Columbus, Ohio, metro region, central-city dwellers were found to be more concerned with the environment and substandard housing, while education and transportation were deemed more critical by suburbanites.[11] Another study of metro areas in Wisconsin found that suburbanites were more willing to forgo the expense of building water and sewer systems and instead preferred to rely on septic tanks and wells.[12] The parallels between these findings and Clark County are interesting to consider when we look at the significant reliance on septic systems and wells in the county versus the city of Springfield's advanced water and sewer systems.

The Wittenberg study identified thirty-nine local government units in Clark County that produced fifty-seven different taxing districts. This situation is pretty typical of Ohio and of most states in the northern United States, which were heavily influenced by the New England tradition of independent local governments. Many states in the southern and southwestern United States had fewer local government units because they had been influenced more by the tradition of southern plantations than by that of New England towns. The overall conclusion that emerged from this analysis was that Clark County was fairly typical of metro counties in Ohio and in the United States. What about the relationship between fragmentation and Springfield's relative elasticity? Based upon the methodology Rusk had used in his earlier book, he placed Springfield in the category of low elasticity. While we found Springfield to be more elastic in tax base, our data agreed with this finding in relation to population. We assumed that this undoubtedly was due in part to the resistance to annexation over the years by townships. However, the data we gathered did not allow us to test this last assumption.

Springfield is typical of most American cities in that new development is occurring on their edges. Springfield is typical of most cities in the Midwest and Northeast in that this new development has usually been outside of the political boundaries of the city. Springfield has two advantages in dealing with this reality. No suburban area has incorporated itself as a city, and Springfield has the only public water and sewer utilities in its immediate area. Finally, typical of all American cities, most new housing is being built in the suburbs for upper-income people, which in turn, leads to the decline of older urban neighborhoods. In metropolitan areas experiencing population growth, these older neighborhoods are becoming home to new residents often from outside the United States. In those metropolitan areas with little or no population growth, these older neighborhoods have become places of abandoned houses or vacant lots. Finally, Springfield is typical of most metropolitan areas—especially inelastic ones, according to Rusk—in that those living in the suburbs do not consider the problems of inner-city neighborhoods to be their problems.

ENACTING RUSK'S RECOMMENDATIONS

Of Rusk's three recommendations, the first two—win-win annexation and comprehensive land-use planning—were directly aimed at this problem of elasticity. At this point politics intervened. Two commissioners decided not to run for reelection in 1997. I was reelected along with two strong new commissioners, Martin Mahoney and Dan Martin, and I was named mayor again. At the top of my agenda was trying to move forward on the proposals coming out of the Rusk process.

One Rusk recommendation was easy. The city joined the county and the regional transportation planning group to fund consultants to produce a land-use plan. They worked through much of 1998 producing a plan for the entire county that was adopted by the city and county commissions. It called for locating housing near public utilities instead of scattering it across the rural area and for designating areas for commercial and industrial development. If followed precisely, this plan would require most development around Springfield to be located on city utilities and thus subject to annexation to the city. Creating a land-use plan is not that difficult; using it to make decisions is. Property owners want to get as much value out of their land as possible. When a farmer wants to subdivide a few lots to send a child to college, it is hard for public bodies to vote no based upon a land-use plan. This was particularly true of the county bodies that made decisions about property outside of the city. Yet the plan stands as a clear guide.

THE COMPREHENSIVE ECONOMIC
DEVELOPMENT AGREEMENT

The Rusk recommendation for win-win annexation is a story all its own. Prime-Ohio is the industrial park developed by the Community Improvement Corporation (CIC) that produced the most new jobs for Springfield in the 1980s and 1990s. By the mid-1990s, the original park was nearly full, so the CIC developed plans for PrimeOhio Two right next door to the original. There was one problem. With the addition of Dole's lettuce-in-a-bag operation, the sewer serving the area had reached capacity. PrimeOhio is on the southeast corner of Springfield, and the Springfield wastewater treatment facility is on the southwest corner. The sewer running through the east side of Springfield from Prime-Ohio was a continuing problem. Since it took rainwater from many of our older neighborhoods, it exceeded capacity when it rained hard. The Environmental Protection Agency did not look kindly upon this. So there were a number of good reasons to build a new sewer line to serve both the current and new Prime-Ohio. The route that made the most sense ran around Springfield on the south, almost totally in Springfield Township. For years, Springfield Township had been the loudest opponent of annexation. We were faced with a challenge that also was an opportunity to try out Rusk's win-win annexation idea.

In the mid-1980s, the CIC had brought the city, county, and township together to produce PrimeOhio; they assumed the same approach would be required again. When CIC approached the city, we suggested a broader approach. We wanted an agreement, at least for the area along the route of the sewer pipe, that would allow annexation. The PrimeOhio agreement required the city to share 5 percent of its income tax with the township. We were willing to discuss a higher level of sharing, but we wanted to include a much larger area than just PrimeOhio Two. Given the findings of the Wittenberg study, we also urged the inclusion of some form of revenue sharing between the two school districts. The CIC began meeting with each of the interested parties. Since the parties were unable or unwilling to deal directly with each other the first time around, the CIC assumed that would be true this time, too. Springfield Township had lost a string of annexation battles and had been unsuccessful in getting the county to develop a suburban utility system. The city held the trump cards: the only public water and sewer systems near the city. Homes built near each other and nearly all commercial and industrial property needed to be connected to public utilities. The township government decided to negotiate, and we quickly agreed with them to share 10 to 15 percent of our income tax revenue from newly annexed areas with township government. We then suggested to the CIC that the city and township meet directly to work out the details. The CIC thought it also had worked out a revenue-sharing agreement among the school districts. Basically, it called for Springfield City Schools to give up all claim to past development, mostly PrimeOhio, in return for an equal share of the tax base that developed after the agreement. The school superintendents agreed to present this to their respective boards of education. Springfield City Schools agreed, but Springfield Local Schools (later Springfield Shawnee) did not.

We discovered a mechanism that provided a framework for a city-township agreement. At the urging of some communities in northern Ohio, Ohio had passed a law allowing for economic development districts between cities and townships. Our local representatives to the Ohio General Assembly were able to amend this law to allow generally for what we were trying to do. We learned that county and state officials were enthusiastic about us working out our own annexation issues without putting them in the middle. When the meetings began, we learned once again that the devil is in the details. Over many months, we met in turn with each of the three Springfield Township trustees. Annexation was to be triggered by the need for utilities; those who did not want utilities did not need to annex. Slowly, we came to understand that the trustees perceived that their biggest political problem was forcing their current residents to annex to the city to get utilities. By the end of the negotiations, the most significant concession the city made to get an agreement was to allow existing residential properties to receive utilities connected to the city system without annexing to the city. In the end, we also agreed to negotiate a second agreement to cover the rest of the township, to establish a common utility rate for the entire township, and to develop some joint control over zoning. In return, the township agreed to allow strings, narrow strips of land connecting the city to properties beyond current residential, in order to meet the Ohio requirement that annexed land be connected to the already existing city. The agreement was reduced to a draft legal document to be voted upon by the city commission, the county commission, and the Springfield Township trustees. One big loose end remained. When the Springfield Local Board of Education refused to share revenue with Springfield City Schools, the township trustees met with them and concluded that it was necessary to eliminate any reference to schools from the agreement. The city manager and I met with Springfield City Schools to explain this and to promise that our commitment to school revenue sharing outside of this agreement remained firm. We return to this topic later.

During May 1999, the city, county, and township voted to adopt the first Comprehensive Economic Development Agreement (CEDA) in Ohio. We had a public signing of the agreement on December 8, 1999. It had taken two years to get done, but this was even more than Rusk had hoped for from win-win annexation. For once, a consultant's visit had actually produced significant public policy. In the past, property owners learned that they needed water and sewer to develop property, and only the city had it. When they approached the city, they learned that they had to be annexed by the city to get the utilities. When the township learned about this situation, they often urged the property owners not to be annexed and fought the annexations, especially before the county commission. When the annexation was complete, the city withdrew the property from the township. Under CEDA, city and township representatives encouraged property owners to be annexed, and the city does not withdraw the property from the township and shares its property tax revenue with the township. This level of cooperation was a very new world for Clark County.

We had accomplished something historic; the Clark County Leadership Association named a township trustee, a county commissioner, and me as their Leaders of the Year. Besides the obvious public achievement, the CEDA process produced some more subtle results. First and foremost, a Springfield city government that had been a laughingstock in Ohio and especially in our region now was recognized as an innovator. Cities and townships around Ohio contacted us and Springfield Township to learn about this imaginative solution to the annexation wars being waged across the state. Springfield's bruised self-image very much needed that recognition. For years, the story of how the CIC had had to drag the public bodies into the PrimeOhio agreement in spite of their obstinate and short-sighted stubbornness was widely told in the local community, especially in business circles. Now we politicians had proved that we could look beyond personalities and immediate interests to produce something that promised to change the future of the entire region for the better. Finally, it is hard to overstate the change this new cooperation created in the relationships among the leaders of the local governments. When you have bargained hard, given each other what was needed for agreement, stepped out side by side in support of the product, stood up to some angry opponents together, and then voted in public, you establish trust and mutual respect that last for a while. Nothing binds people to each other more than thinking that they have made a little history together.

Chapter 3

Wilson's Concentration of Poverty Divides Springfield

In his discussion of concentration of poverty, William Julius Wilson brings us back from the edge of the city to its center, especially to its older and poorer neighborhoods.[1] He begins by recognizing an increase in negative indicators in these neighborhoods; violent crime and single-parent families are the two he emphasizes. Both have gone up significantly in recent decades in the neighborhoods he examined. Wilson suggests that an increasing concentration of poverty helps explain the growth in these problems. He used census data from Chicago to show that with each decade those neighborhoods that started out with larger-than-usual percentages of poor people had dramatic increases in the percentages of poor people. For example, a census tract that had 5 percent poor in 1960 might have 10 percent poor by 1970, 25 percent by 1980, 40 percent by 1990, and 60 percent by 2000. Chicago had always had neighborhoods that were poorer than others, but until some time in the 1960s even the poorer neighborhoods still had a large number of people who were not poor living there. We might call this old-style neighborhood a "composite neighborhood," made up of people of various incomes. Census data from these Chicago neighborhoods also indicate that the census tracts with large increases of poverty also experienced dramatic declines in their total population. The obvious conclusion is that the percentage of people who were poor went up not because poor people moved in but because those who could afford to do so moved out.

Since most of the high-poverty neighborhoods in Chicago were primarily African American, Wilson assumed that the breakdown of racial segregation was key. He reasoned that African Americans who could have afforded to move to less poor neighborhoods earlier but were prevented from doing so by racial segregation took the opportunity to move when segregation ended. Left behind were neighborhoods composed mostly of people who could not afford to move. In contemporary America, poor families are usually young families with young children and often with only one parent and senior citizens. The children of these neighborhoods usually face the disadvantage of growing up in a family with limited resources, but, according to Wilson, increasingly they also face a neighborhood with fewer resources to help them succeed than an affluent or middle-income neighborhood, or even an old composite urban neighborhood. Wilson emphasized three weaknesses of these neighborhoods: lack of role models, weakened networks of human relations, and deteriorating community institutions.

FUNCTIONAL COMPOSITE NEIGHBORHOODS

I grew up in an old composite urban neighborhood in Silvis, Illinois. We were nearly all white and mostly blue-collar, but on the one hand we had a few people we considered well off and on the other hand we had some families on welfare or very close to it. Those children who had only one parent or no parent who worked regularly lived next door or down the block from neighbors or even relatives who worked full-time or lived in a stable, two-parent family. Role models of the discipline of work, of home ownership, of loving marriage, of faithful church going, of commitment to education, and of at least some economic success were on all sides. While neither of my parents graduated from high school, near us lived a high school physics teacher who coached baseball. That looked like a pretty good life to me. Contemporary high-poverty neighborhoods are composed primarily of single-parent families, children and youth, and older people, all of whom are economically unable to move out. Stable, middle-aged adults, the role models of the past, are exactly those who have left.

Two people we considered important lived on my block in Silvis. Hap Weekley was a superintendent at a local International plant that made combines; he had three daughters, one about the same age as each of us Copeland boys. Harold "Chappie" Chapman was the vice president at the Silvis National Bank, who went out on the back porch of his house and fired a shotgun in the air every New Year's Eve. In the old composite neighborhoods, although some parents did not have direct connections who could help their children get ahead, they did have indirect connections through social networks. Next door or down the block or at church, they knew someone who could vouch for them with a first employer or help them get a loan they needed. My oldest brother, Bob, dated the oldest of the three Weekley girls; Hap may have liked him better than she did. In any event, when Bob needed a first job, he found it at Hap's combine plant. Years later, when Bob needed a first mortgage on a little house, he got it through Chappie Chapman. Middle- and upper-income people rely on such networks so much that we often do not even notice them. These networks are frayed in contemporary, high-poverty neighborhoods. Young people in these neighborhoods may have their own networks, called "gangs" by the rest of us, through which they can get in trouble. They are less likely to have the connections they need to get ahead in the mainstream because those who had those connections have left.

In the old composite neighborhoods, schools worked for most students, churches with resources served their neighborhoods, local businesses provided services and jobs, and parks and community centers provided recreation. Young people got the education they needed to get ahead, found friends and inspiration in their church youth group, secured their first job with the neighborhood business, and hung out at the local park or community center. As I grew up in Silvis, I attended an elementary school for kindergarten through eighth grade that drew its students from families of factory workers and some professionals and some poor kids. While we had no African American kids, we had a number of Mexican kids from Second, Third, and Fourth streets. The school was well ordered, frugally but adequately funded, and supported by a very strong PTA. The Southern Baptist, Methodist, and Catholic churches were major forces in the community. I spent my summers at the Silvis Park, playing baseball and cards, or at McKinley grade school, playing basketball without incidents. Mom and I walked down the hill to buy groceries in downtown Silvis; we rode the bus to Moline or East Moline to shop for clothes and shoes. Community institutions functioned fairly well for me and my neighbors.

In the contemporary urban poverty neighborhood, businesses close, replaced by fast-food restaurants, rent-to-own and used furniture stores, and check cashing places. Schools deteriorate; even the best teachers are severely challenged when nearly every child in their classes comes from a poor family without much educational experience. Churches, composed mostly of poor people, struggle valiantly to meet their people's needs. Parks frequently have become drug hangouts, and many community centers have closed. Wilson emphasized most the loss of work when businesses close and the jobs move to the suburbs beyond public transportation.

The picture Wilson paints is stark indeed, yet all of the facts of the growing disparities between rich and poor in our society are testimony to the realities he discusses. In an economy that increasingly requires education to get a good job, these contemporary poor city neighborhoods produce young people unlikely to succeed but very likely to become major problems for the cities in which they live. Has poverty become more concentrated in Springfield? How is race involved in the answer? The future of many of Springfield's neighborhoods may depend on the answers to these questions and on what we do on the basis of those answers.

CONCENTRATION OF POVERTY IN SPRINGFIELD

Since Wilson's analysis assumes that race is key to the phenomena of concentration of poverty, the Wittenberg urban studies team first examined the extent of racial segregation in Springfield.[2] Census data for Springfield shows that there was some limited desegregation between 1970 and 1980, most of it due to the construction of an isolated low-income housing project in the white middle-income northeastern corner of the city. Little changed between 1980 and 1990. Over this twenty-year period, racial change mostly meant that neighborhoods already with significant African American populations became more African American and that areas bordering upon these neighborhoods gained in African American population. The 2000 Census showed the continuation of these trends. For instance, the Southgate neighborhood that was 70 percent white in 1980 was 50 percent white by 1990 and 70 percent African American by 2000. Springfield remains a very racially segregated city. When the areas just outside the city are factored in, the picture is even worse. Census tracts bordering the city range from 97 percent to 100 percent white. Race clearly divides our neighborhoods.

Most American cities have higher concentrations of poor people than their surrounding suburban areas, which places bigger demands upon city governments as they try to meet the additional needs of their poor citizens. Cities that are experiencing a declining tax base and a higher percentage of poor citizens find that they have fewer and fewer resources to try to do something about bigger and bigger problems. Poor persons depend much more on public services, everything from bus service to housing inspection to drinking water and sewers, than those with more money who can afford cars, good housing, and wells and septic systems. One way Rusk has approached this problem is with his concept of the fair share of poverty. He believes it would be fairest if poverty were shared more or less equally across a metropolitan area; full equality in amount of poverty would produce a score of 100 on what he calls the fair share of poverty index. The higher the number, the more the burden of poverty is borne by the city. Springfield's score is 176, slightly better than the 192 score for all of Ohio's cities, but higher than the average for North Carolina cities (124). On this as with most of Rusk's other measures of how healthy a city is, Springfield tends to fall somewhere between healthy Columbus and unhealthy Cleveland and Dayton.

We then turned directly to an examination of Wilson's concept of concentration of poverty in Springfield. Data showed that within the city of Springfield, we were concentrating more and more those who were poor. This was certainly true in Springfield's traditionally African American southwestern area. With each census, the percentage of people who were poor by official standards had increased in these tracts. Again, this was typical of American cities. Between 1970 and 1990, there had been a 118 percent increase in the number of African American people living in tracts with higher than 30 percent poverty rates in the United States. Springfield followed Wilson's Chicago pattern, but it also added to Wilson's analysis. If we looked at the census results for 1970, 1980, 1990, and

2000, we saw just what Wilson found in Chicago. Tracts that were less than 20 percent poor in 1970 moved over that line by 2000; those that were 20 percent poor in 1970 were over 40 percent poor by 2000. The concentration of poverty deepened and widened with each decade. What is different in Springfield is that our poorest census tract (census tract 3 in the Selma Road area) is largely white. As in the country at large, we have more poor white people than poor African American people in Springfield. While 33 percent of African American Springfielders were poor, 18 percent of whites were poor. However, since whites make up more than 80 percent of the city's population, there are four times as many poor whites as poor African Americans in Springfield.

Across America, the African American poor are concentrated; around 75 percent live in neighborhoods with 20 percent or more poor. On the other hand, the white poor mostly live in neighborhoods that are not poor; only around 25 percent live in neighborhoods with 20 percent or more poor. If Wilson is right about the differences between poor and composite neighborhoods, this difference between the African American poor and white poor nationally is very significant because opportunity is so much greater in composite neighborhoods, which means that poor whites are more likely to get ahead than poor African Americans. In the 1990 census, Springfield followed the national trend for our African American poor; 75.2 percent lived in neighborhoods with 20 percent or more poor. However, in Springfield our white poor were also concentrated; 53.8 percent of the white poor lived in neighborhoods that were 20 percent or more poor. This situation provided us with a golden research opportunity in Springfield. We could look at whether the concentration of poor whites seemed to produce the same results as the concentration of poor African Americans. In our research about neighborhoods, focused on crime and schools, we found that problems did not relate to race as much as to income. This did not mean that African Americans in Springfield were better off than elsewhere, so much as that a large portion of poor whites were about as badly off here. This was, and is, a major challenge for our community.

FIVE NEIGHBORHOODS

Since the census data is so massive, and numbers lack flesh and blood, we chose five census tracts within the city to try to bring life to the numbers.[3] We did not claim that they were typical or represented all city neighborhoods, but they did represent a wide range of racial and economic realities. We also chose six census areas outside the city not for contrast among themselves but rather for some comparison to the city tracts. To facilitate comparison of census and school data, we chose our tracts so that they corresponded roughly to elementary schools. The primary purpose of the detailed analysis of these census tracts was to examine in greater depth in Springfield the issues raised by William Julius Wilson. For this reason, we chose two census tracts that were high in poverty, one (Selma Road)

Table 3.1. Springfield's Census Tracts, 1990

Census Tract Number	Neighborhood Name	Elementary School	Population	% White	Median Family Income	% Poor	% Very Poor	% Less than High School Education	Median House Values
3	Selma Road	Emerson	2,502	86	$13,045	40	20	58	$22,200
9.02	South Yellow Springs	Fulton	1,077	23	$16,542	39	23	53	$30,300
11.02	Southgate	Perrin Woods	3,416	50	$28,056	11	4	32	$40,500
13	Kenwood Heights	Kenwood	4,801	96	$24,025	13	4	35	$40,300
18	Ridgewood	Snowhill	3,864	95	$36,196	6	1	18	$65,700
20	Forest Hills	Rockway	2,189	99	$40,212	3	1	13	$71,300
22	Shawnee	Reid	4,426	97	$36,038	9	3	25	$71,000
25	German Township	Northwestern	3,371	99	$31,360	4	1	23	$69,400
33.02	Madison Township	Miami View	2,472	98	$22,863	13	4	29	$51,000
23.02 (part)	Northridge (N)	Northridge	1,297	98	$45,509	2	0	15	$69,500
24.01 (part)	Northridge (S)	Northridge	4,642	100	$35,184	3	3	23	$63,100
Springfield			70,487	82	$21,407	21	10	32	$41,200
Clark County			147,548	90	$27,743	13	6	27	$53,900

Table 3.2. Springfield's Census Tracts, 2000

Census Tract Number	Neighborhood Name	Elementary School	Population	% White	Median Family Income	% Poor	% Very Poor	% Less than High School Education	Median House Values
3	Selma Road	Emerson	2,004	69	$23,424	37	19	51	$36,900
9.02	South Yellow Springs	Fulton	1,381	No data	$32,150	18	14	24	$53,000
11.02	Southgate	Perrin Woods	3,117	29	$52,366	10	6	18	$64,000
13	Kenwood Heights	Kenwood	4,352	94	$42,480	8	4	24	$65,000
18	Ridgewood	Snowhill	3,771	91	$52,250	6	4	12	$97,200
20	Forest Hills	Rockway	2,265	99	$61,667	5	2	10	$116,000
22	Shawnee	Reid	4,714	95	$61,181	5	3	13	$119,400
25	German Township	Northwestern	5,373	96	$53,139	5	2	20	$101,800
33.02	Madison Township	Miami View	2,796	97	$50,954	22	6	20	$90,500
23.02 (part)	Northridge (N)	Northridge	4,337	97	$59,440	2	0	7	$118,800
24.01 (part)	Northridge (S)	Northridge	8,835	95	$55,156	5	2	11	$105,200
Springfield			65,322	78	$39,890	30	13	23	$69,600
Clark County			144,742	88	$48,259	11	4	19	$90,500

populated primarily by whites of Appalachian roots and one (South Yellow Springs) populated primarily by African Americans. We also chose two neighborhoods that were middle income, one (Kenwood Heights) that was predominantly white and one (Southgate) that was around half African American. There was not a middle-income, predominantly African American neighborhood in 1990 (but Southgate was 70 percent African American by 2000). Finally, we chose the most affluent census tract within the city (Ridgewood); there was no neighborhood of comparative affluence that had a significant number of African Americans. The census tracts outside the city represented those that ringed the city and one small town and rural area that did not border on the city.

Except for race, Selma Road (census tract 3) and South Yellow Springs (census tract 9.02) looked about the same. The people of both had low incomes; about 40 percent of the population of each tract lived in families below the federal poverty level, double the figure for the city as a whole. Between 25 and 30 percent of the families were on public assistance. Six or seven out of ten of the children under five years of age were living in families that were poor. More than half of the adults in the neighborhood had failed to graduate from high school, and nearly none had graduated from college. Rental housing was relatively cheap, but people had to spend a big portion of their incomes on it. Housing had a very low value. In sum, these two neighborhoods were very typical of low-income neighborhoods in other cities in America such as those Wilson described. Except for race, Kenwood Heights (census tract 13) and Southgate (census tract 11.02) were much the same. Both were marked by moderate incomes near the average for the city and by levels of poverty that were about half that of the city at large. Only about one in ten families received public assistance, and even children under five years of age were unlikely to live in poor families. Most adults had graduated from high school, and many had attended college. Rental properties were somewhat more expensive than in the low-income neighborhoods, but renters had to pay a smaller share of their income on rent. Housing averaged nearly twice as much value as in the Selma Road and South Yellow Springs neighborhoods. These two tracts were typical of the middle-income neighborhoods of Springfield like the old composite urban neighborhoods in cities across America. Ridgewood was typical of three or four other neighborhoods on the north side of Springfield with few residents who were poor or not white. Almost all of the people living in these neighborhoods had graduated from high school, and a majority attended college. Similar neighborhoods can be found in most American cities.

THE SUBURBAN CENSUS TRACTS

Ringing the city of Springfield is a whole series of residential subdivisions that remain in the unincorporated county. Usually the housing within each of these subdivisions is of a similar size, style, and cost. Given the big differences we saw among the census tracts inside the city, what is most obvious about the five suburban census tracts was how much they were alike according to the 1990 census. They ranged from 97 percent to 100 percent white, more white than any of the city tracts. Median household income ranged from about five thousand dollars below Ridgewood to almost ten thousand dollars above Ridgewood. All were dramatically higher than the other four tracts inside the city. In fact, the median income for the entire city was almost ten thousand dollars lower than the lowest of the suburban tracts. There were pockets of low-income population in almost all of these suburban areas. The level of poverty in these census tracts ranged from 2 percent to 9 percent, but the census tracts were large enough that these pockets get lost when they are averaged into the tract data. The Madison Township census tract is more rural than suburban; it has population characteristics quite comparable to those of the Kenwood tract in the city, except for race.

SCHOOLS

In order to explore Wilson's theory that neighborhoods with high concentrations of poverty produce serious social problems, we examined schools and crime, two primary reasons that people give for moving out of cities. Ohio schools are subject to a series of proficiency tests designed to indicate the level of achievement in each school. They are also required to report serious disciplinary action—physical restraints and suspensions. When we examined this and some other data[4] available from the Ohio Department of Education homepage[5] for elementary schools, we found that it did vary with the income levels of the neighborhoods served by those schools. The five census tracts within the city we chose to analyze were picked in part because they related to five very different elementary schools: Emerson (Selma Road), Fulton (South Yellow Springs), Perrin Woods (Southgate), Kenwood (Kenwood Heights), and Snowhill (Ridgewood). These elementary schools represented well the diversity of education experiences available within Springfield City Schools. First, we should note some general characteristics about the district. In 1995, Springfield City Schools enrolled 11,376 students, down from 12,076 in 1986; the enrollment has continued to decline since. Of these students, 71.3 percent were counted as white and 28.7 percent as nonwhite.

A few general facts about our five city schools were immediately apparent. First, the schools were less racially segregated than their neighborhoods; Springfield City Schools had entered into an agreement with the federal government back in the 1970s to integrate its schools by redrawing its district lines and by allowing students to transfer between schools if doing so would improve racial balance. This led to racial mixing primarily between low-income students in redrawn Southside districts and between smaller numbers of African American students whose parents chose to transfer them to primarily white Northside schools. Second, as college-level educators, we could not imagine the extremely high mobility rate in the low-income schools, where as many as half of the students would change during a school year. Third, the free-lunch numbers suggested that the school populations reflect the income levels of their neighborhoods very closely. Then there were the test scores that varied with the income levels of their neighborhoods. Ten percent or less passed all parts of the tests in the low-income schools; results for the middle-income schools were in the thirties; Snowhill at 84 percent had the highest scores in Clark County. Finally, discipline reports showed the same relationship, suggesting that the principals of schools serving low-income students spent a great deal of their time on discipline while principals of schools serving upper-income students were free to focus on learning. There is no reason to believe that there has been any change in the relationship between income and test scores and discipline since this study.

It should be no surprise that Snowhill was the award-winning school in Springfield. Who would doubt that students sitting in a Snowhill classroom are much more likely to graduate from college and thus succeed in today's economy than those sitting in the classrooms of any of the other four schools? The results from these five schools—Emerson, Fulton, Perrin Woods, Kenwood, and Snowhill—showed that the income level, not the race of the families from which the students came, was key. Emerson was mostly white, and Fulton was mostly black; Kenwood was mostly white, and Perrin Woods was more black than white. Racial composition did not seem to make much difference, but the income level of the schools clearly did. What set Snowhill apart was not the race of its students but rather the financial and educational resources of their parents.

For the sake of comparison, we briefly examined the elementary schools serving our county census tracts that are outside of the city. As with the city schools, the proficiency scores of elementary schools varied according to the median income of the census tract served by those elementary schools. The county school with the lowest scores was just somewhat above Springfield's middle-income city schools. The county schools with the highest scores were somewhat below the highest scores among the city schools. As in the city, the proficiency tests seemed to be a better measure of the economic makeup of the parts of the community served by the schools than of the quality of instruction in the various schools. Discipline records for the 1995–96 school year for county schools outside of the city suggested that a much more orderly learning environment existed there than in many city schools. The data suggested that students who attend schools serving mostly low-income children face major hurdles to their education compared to those who attended schools that serve higher-income neighborhoods. There were fewer academically able students to challenge them and to learn with them. Their learning situation was less orderly, and their teachers and administrators had less time for instruction because they had to deal with discipline much of the time. Still, good teaching and good learning were going on in every one of the schools we studied.

This situation has significance for school funding also. If we truly believe that no child should be left behind, we are going to have to provide additional help to low-income schools in order to help their kids achieve better, which has implica-

Table 3.3. Basic Facts about Springfield's City Schools, 1995–96 School Year

School	Students	Percent White	Mobility	Free Lunch	Passed All Parts of Fourth-Grade Test	Suspensions and Physical Restraint	Proficiency Tests 2001–2
Emerson	536	69.6	54%	84.1%	10	97	25.0
Fulton	415	60.5	41%	88.3%	7	68	25.0
Kenwood	407	70.3	27%	50.0%	39	28	45.0
Perrin Woods	334	52.4	23%	58.2%	32	3	54.6
Snowhill	470	78.3	15%	21.3%	84	2	82.4

tions for funding within an urban district like Springfield City Schools. On average, students attending Snowhill require less help than those attending Fulton in order to succeed. Thinking on a metropolitan basis, this is even truer when comparing urban schools to suburban schools. We are simply going to have to spend more money to educate successfully students from families with less money and education. I return to this matter in a later chapter dealing with schools.

CRIME

Besides the quality of schools, safety stands as a critical factor in the quality of life in a neighborhood.[7] We wanted to find out whether the crime data supported the view that the degree of safety is very different in different neighborhoods. Some cautions about crime statistics apply here. People may have been more likely to report crime in some neighborhoods than others. Different recording practices are less likely because the same police agency was involved for them all. Differences in reporting procedures raise serious questions about comparing different communities. In this case, a different problem arose. The Springfield Police Division recorded the number and type of 911 calls for different police districts. We attempted to match those districts to census tracts. In those cases where the census tracts and police precincts did not match up, estimates and approximations connected the 911 calls to a specific census tract. It is also worth noting that the data suggested that crime was not simply a problem in residential areas. The neighborhood with by far the most 911 calls was census tract 1, which is the downtown area. It is unlikely that these calls came from those who lived there as much as from those who visited. Gathering places such as bars were primary sources of 911 calls for crimes like disorderly conduct. A look at our census tracts showed the trends we expected, but less dramatically than we might have thought. Selma Road, our lowest-income neighborhood, had the highest numbers, about five times as large as those of higher-income neighborhoods. However, Southgate's calls were closer in number to those of Ridgewood than we might have expected, and Kenwood's were actually higher than those of South Yellow Springs. In sum, the income levels of census tracts explained about half of the difference in 911 calls. Interestingly, 911 calls were lower in our African American tracts than in comparable white tracts. Reported crime in Selma Road was much higher than in South Yellow Springs, and it was higher in Kenwood than in Southgate. There was a relationship between the income level of a census tract and the number of 911 police calls from that tract. Low-income neighborhoods produced more calls than neighborhoods of higher income. However, higher percentages of African Americans in a census tract simply did not predict higher numbers of 911 police calls from that tract.

Crime was lower outside the city but increasing there, too. When we turned to a comparison between city and suburban county crime data, we immediately ran into some differences in methods of reporting and the fact that we only had access to data from the sheriff's office. While the rate of violent crime in the nation's fifty-two largest cities increased 33 percent between 1979 and 1989, suburban crime rates increased by only 14 percent. Nationally, suburban crime rates were roughly 25 percent of city rates and are increasing at a slower rate. The differences between Springfield and the outside county were not nearly that far apart, but the city did outpace the outside county in all seven categories of serious offenses. This increase undoubtedly reflected some changes in the procedure for maintaining crime statistics in the sheriff's office, and these figures were only for a selected period of time. However, these numbers did suggest that violent crimes had increased in the county. Interestingly, the largest percentage of crime calls in Clark County came from lower-income areas that had a large number of trailer parks.

KEY FINDINGS ABOUT NEIGHBORHOODS

Many people who lived in Springfield during the time we are studying thought that the Southside was poor and African American. In fact, our poorest neighborhood was mostly white, there were four times as many poor whites as poor African Americans in Clark County, and, unlike most metropolitan areas, much white poverty was concentrated poverty here. On the other hand, Southgate was a middle-income neighborhood in the southwestern quadrant of the city, a surprise to most Northsiders. The numbers confirmed what Wilson said and most people thought; school test scores were lower, and 911 calls were higher in low-income neighborhoods. Concentrated poverty, not race, seemed to be the reason, slightly amending Wilson's conclusions. The system of school funding and annexation policies in Ohio produced major inequities in the tax base among schools, which was getting significantly worse as people moved to the suburbs. Finally, there were a lot of local governments in Clark County, sometimes antagonistic with one another and often uncoordinated. None of these findings was inconsistent with the basic analyses of Rusk and Wilson. Sadly in this case, Springfield was very typical of urban America.

The last of Rusk's recommendations—on housing dispersal—turned out to be impossible. Our state representative had legislation drafted to enact Rusk's housing dispersal ideas at the state level and introduced it. He was not able to get action on it before he was eliminated by term limits, and no one in the Ohio General Assembly has picked up on it since. Thus, in Springfield as in other cities, life is very different depending upon where you live. Geography not only reflects the inequalities present in metropolitan areas but also threatens to produce a future that not only perpetuates those divisions but even deepens them. In an economy that increasingly ties opportunity to education and in a society in which education is as tied to where people live as we found in Springfield, children will be left behind. This, the clearest example of the injustice that divides metropolitan areas in contemporary America, is the issue that we clearly identified in our analysis of Springfield, and the issue that sets the agenda for the rest of this book.

THE LOCAL SCENE CHANGES

About this time, three other big changes occurred on the local scene. New leadership in the Chamber of Commerce led to a much more active program for the chamber and revived the CIC's role in economic development. For two decades, the former president of the Chamber of Commerce saw his job as selling dirt, attracting new employers to town. New leadership has led to a much more active program of services for chamber members and a new emphasis on branding and public relations aimed at improving Springfield's image. The chamber has now turned to becoming much more active in economic development.

Another major new development began with the death of Harry Turner, a local insurance executive who helped found the quite successful Cincinnati Insurance Company. Upon his death, the Turner Foundation was born, with the purpose of improving life in Springfield and Clark County. The foundation has assets sufficient to make it a major actor in Springfield. A grandson, John Landess, returned from Nashville to head the new foundation. Landess soon gathered around him a group of people committed to using the resources of the Turner Foundation to bring a new day to Springfield. Their commitments to downtown redevelopment, striking design, and historic preservation were placed within an overarching drive to attract people of means to Springfield. In time, this led them into economic development, with a preference for cutting-edge businesses that paid good wages. They settled particularly on information technology.

The third new development had to do with our member of the U.S. House of Representatives, David Hobson. Matt and I had worked closely with him on a number of projects, especially two separate successful efforts to keep an Air National Guard unit at our municipal airport. Dave and I had come to respect and trust each other, even given our partisan differences. By 2000, he had worked his way up to be the chair of a subcommittee of the Appropriations Committee. In Washington, chairs of subcommittees of the Appropriations Committee are called "cardinals" and are able to designate various funds for projects in their home districts. All of a sudden, we had a source of significant pork. Soon the folks back home figured this out. The first really big project that our connection brought to Springfield was Lexis/Nexis. Lexis/Nexis is one of the two most commonly used computer legal research sources in the world. Their primary location was south of Dayton. They were looking for a backup location close enough to drive to but far enough away that it likely would not be hit by the same tornado or other service interruption. With $5 million from the federal government because of Dave Hobson and additional financial support from the Turner Foundation, Lexis/Nexis promised not even to look elsewhere. With guarantees from the city and the county, the deal was struck, and the facility built. With additional dollars secured from the federal government by Dave Hobson, a technology park was built next door to Lexis/Nexis. A cardinal who loves his hometown can make a lot of things possible. However, in 2007 he announced that he would not seek reelection.

A change to the city's charter required that the mayor be elected directly by the people, starting with the 2003 municipal election. I won with 64 percent of the vote in November 2003, becoming the first directly elected mayor of Springfield in ninety years. I was safely mayor for four more years, and ran unopposed for reelection in 2007.

ALL-AMERICA CITY

In 2003, Springfield was chosen as one of thirty finalists for the National Civic League's All-America City program, from which ten cities would be named All-America Cities in May 2003 in Washington, D.C. We put together a team to make our presentation, wrote a script, assembled large pictures, and raised money. We went to Washington, made our case, and answered the judges' questions superbly. We knew we had won, but when they announced the ten winning cities, they somehow forgot us. When I spoke as a part of the parade of spokespersons for each of the losers, I said that, when we went home, our story was that we finished tied for eleventh and that we were sticking to it, and we urged the others not in the top ten to do the same.

We came home, wrote a new application, and resubmitted the following year. Again chosen as a finalist, we decided to humanize our presentation by adding Larry Coleman, a local African American minister, who sang with some members of his choir. Again, we thought we had won, and this time the judges agreed with us. Springfield was one of ten All-America Cities for 2004. I came home to explain that being an All-America City does not mean that you are one of the ten fastest-growing or wealthiest or prettiest cities in the United States. It means that you are a city recognized for facing its problems and working together to deal with them. That is the truth about the award and about Springfield.

In fifteen years, Springfield had gone from a city in deep despair to an All-America City. We had continued to lose population to the suburbs and lose jobs to automation and places with lower wages; we had continued to have high levels of poverty and neighborhoods under stress. Yet we had come to believe in ourselves and in our city government enough to work together to confront these challenges. Certainly, I had learned a lot along the way, much of which found its way into my ethics classes.

In the next part of this book, I share my ethical, religious, and theological reflections upon this experience in hopes that they will help us think ethically about cities in the United States today. I begin these reflections with the conviction that the relationship between our inner cities and our suburbs increasingly is a serious issue of justice in our society. As I explore this conviction further, I will continue to illustrate what I have to say from my Springfield experience. This approach illustrates my fundamental approach to ethics. Some believe that ethics begins with principles, gets them clearly established and defended, and then applies them to specific situations. Others think that ethics is almost totally decided by specific contexts. I begin in the concrete situation, seeking to identify the justice issues present in it, seek to identify principles to help us think about those social issues, and then consider what sort of action flows from that analysis.

With the context of Springfield, Ohio, in mind, we now turn to some ethical, religious, and theological analysis of the experience I have described. Then, in the third part of this book, we turn to the question of what policies can help us create a better urban future. When I continue to refer to Springfield along the way, it is to make ethical principles and religious commitments clearer by seeing their concrete meaning. In so doing, I hope to cause you to think of comparable realities in the cities you know and to come to terms with what I think is a critical ethical challenge for this country: the future of our cities.

PART TWO
ETHICAL AND THEOLOGICAL REFLECTION

Chapter 4

Four Ethical Angles
on the City

Living on the Northside, Southside, Eastside, or Westside tends to provide a very different perspective on Springfield. However, the angle from which we view the world is not primarily a matter of physical location. We also are located socially, politically, and economically. An African American living on the Northside of Springfield may view the world more like an African American living on the Southside than like her Northside neighbors. A political conservative living on the Eastside of Springfield may look at the world more like a political conservative who lives on the Northside than like his Eastside neighbors. A UAW factory worker living on the Westside of Springfield may see the world more like a UAW factory worker on the Southside than like his Westside neighbors. A real person has a unique point of view that is a mixture of these locations and many others, combined in a way that is different from every other person alive.

That said, our society is organized so that these locations are not distributed randomly throughout the population. Persons who are African American or who have lower incomes are much more likely to live on the Southside of Springfield than on the Northside. Every politician who runs for election in Springfield knows that the third ward on the Northside will produce more Republican votes and that the fifth and seventh wards on the Southside will produce mostly

Figure 4.1. Angles on the City

Competitive City	Populist City
Agency = Chamber of Commerce	Agency = CONA
Goal = Jobs	Goal = Good Neighborhoods
Process = Decisive Leadership	Process = Local Control
Value = Economic Well-Being	Value = Empowerment
Vulnerability = Undemocratic and Sacrifice Other Goods	Vulnerability = Legitimacy and Parochialism
Efficient Cause	Material Cause

Pluralist City	Planned City
Agency = Mayor	Agency = David Rusk
Goal = Functioning System	Goal = Rational Development
Process = Participation	Process = Consulting Experts
Value = Balance	Value = Common Good
Vulnerability = Indecision and Unorganized Interests	Vulnerability = Elitism and Lack of Realism
Formal Cause	Final Cause

Democratic votes. It is not an accident that African Americans, lower incomes, and Democratic votes overlap or that Republican votes, higher incomes, and the absence of African Americans do. Again, all African Americans are not low-income people, and all low-income people are not Democrats, but there tends to be a significant correlation.

One more way of looking at the world that mixes in with the physical, social, political, and economic is the ethical. Since I teach religious ethics, it should come as no surprise that I believe our ethical worldviews underlie all of the others and raise the issue of our basic vision of the city. We each have our own unique angle on the world, so there are as many views of Springfield as there are people who live here. However, it can help us think about what difference it makes when we look at the city from a particular angle by identifying basic alternatives and examining them in detail. In doing so, remember that these positions describe ideal types; they are generalizations that describe ways of thinking. They may not perfectly represent the positions of any particular individuals.

The four positions we examine further are the competitive city, the populist city, the pluralist city, and the planned city.[1] In order to make these positions more real, I connect each to actual groups active in Springfield, although this approach is dangerous. I am sure that more than one member of each of these groups accurately could respond, "I don't think like that." That is precisely why so many ethical analyses, political speeches, and sermons are so general that we cannot really tell how they apply to everyday life. So with apologies in advance, I plunge into the specifics in the hope that this discussion will help clarify our thinking and also be more interesting than generalizations with no concrete references.

THE COMPETITIVE CITY

For the Springfield–Clark County Chamber of Commerce, Springfield is one city in direct and tough competition with other cities in and out of Ohio.[2] They see their most essential purpose as attracting and keeping businesses that provide jobs for the people who live in the area. In the struggle to keep International Harvester truck production in Springfield, the chamber formed the Community Improvement Corporation (CIC). Let us review what we know about the CIC. The CIC is a nonprofit corporation whose purpose is to further the economic development of Springfield and Clark County. Its board comprises five representatives of the chamber, two members of the Springfield City Commission, and two members of the Clark County Commission. Using local and state funds, the CIC bought the local International Harvester plant and leased it back to International Harvester to help entice them to stay in town back in 1982. Over a period of years, International Harvester (later Navistar and now International Truck and Engine) bought the plant back.

Out of that success, the CIC launched a broader economic development program in the late 1980s. The most obvious result is PrimeOhio, the premier industrial park in the area. The CIC bought land at an interstate interchange and received some state help for infrastructure, including highway improvements. They then forged an agreement between Springfield and Springfield Township to provide for annexation of the property to the city in return for extension of city water and sewer service. I use the term "forged" very intentionally. Forging involves a lot of heat and some serious hammering, which is exactly what the CIC applied to everyone involved in order to make PrimeOhio happen. This activity had all been completed just before I joined the city commission in 1988. For the CIC, the concerns of the city and township were trivial as compared to the value of the jobs that would be created.

PrimeOhio has been a marvelous success. The eighty-eight acres added in 1996 because the original park was sold out now also are gone, and the last of PrimeOhio became the beginning of the Nextedge Information Technology Park. This development has meant more jobs for the area and additional tax revenue for local government, but a price has been paid for this success. Residents of Springfield have made significant investments, primarily in the form of utilities. Clark County has invested county funds in the project. Springfield Township has received less tax revenue than if annexation had not occurred. Springfield City Schools do not get property taxes from the area because school annexation goes a completely different route than city annexation. Nevertheless, for the chamber, the lesson of PrimeOhio seems clear: the area must compete for jobs, and everyone in the community must cooperate if we are to win that competition.

In a real sense, the chamber thinks of the community as a corporation competing with other corporations for customers, businesses looking to locate jobs here or threatening to move them elsewhere. While we cannot do anything the customer may want, we must do everything we can to offer a better deal than our competitors are offering. I have seen the chamber give up on a prospect because they felt we just could not win that particular competition at a price we could afford, or more accurately that the price was too high for the number and quality of the jobs involved. But that decision comes only after every possibility for improving the deal has been explored, and especially after every possible source of government funds has been tapped.

This approach assumes that the base of a community is economic. Specifically, it considers jobs the single most important reality in people's lives, eliminating or making much easier every other issue they face. Family life, downtown deterioration, housing, schools, and crime all are easier to deal with if people have jobs. The chamber may support social services for families, revitalization of downtown, housing programs, or tax levies for schools or police, but none is as basic as jobs, and in the end support for anything else by the chamber must be justified by how it helps the local economy. If for any reason a choice must be made in the short run between any of these important concerns and jobs, the chamber would choose jobs. As profits are the final test of success for a corporation, jobs saved or added to the local economy are the test of the success of a city.

Those who hold this view of the competitive city tend to apply one other characteristic of the corporate model: someone must be boss. In the past, the chamber, through the CIC, had assumed the role of CEO of this community corporation. The chamber believed that it was best situated to decide what was best for the economic development of the area and that others should follow its lead. Within the CIC in the past, the five chamber members generally knew the key issues to come up in a CIC meeting and usually were in agreement before the meeting began. The four public members, two from the city and two from the county, usually found out about issues before the CIC only as they came up in the meeting and always could be outvoted, if necessary. Other developers or businesspeople who stood in the way of a good deal were considered either uninformed or not team players. Public officials were helpful if they supported the deals or problems if they did not; they deserved support at election time accordingly. In the last few years, as the CIC has run short of resources and has been less effective in attracting and keeping jobs, the process has opened up a bit. Since the CIC has not brought as many new jobs to Springfield recently, some of those who were involved in its successes might argue that greater openness has produced fewer results.

The chamber often saw democratic procedures as necessary evils, at best. They preferred no public discussion of deals until they were nailed down. They preferred to manage the media, refusing to comment until they were ready to announce a final result. Political bodies, at least in Ohio, live in a fishbowl. The state Open Meetings Act requires that the meetings of political bodies be public, except for a few specific topics: purchase or sale of property, some personnel items, labor negotiations, or matters under litigation. Some of what is involved in a typical economic development deal qualifies, but some does not. The news media cover city and county government closely and continually. Most elected officials talk a lot, so it is very difficult for us to keep secret matters that corporate executives just assume are private. The chamber only occasionally appears for public hearings or at meetings of public bodies. They assume that elected officials are responsible for delivering what is needed for the deal.

The positive ethical principle that drives the chamber's view of the city is unified effort for the sake of economic well-being. For advocates of the competitive angle, process is much less important than results, and the particular results that count are jobs. According to this view, business deserves cooperation and support from government and the public because they provide those jobs. Those who do not go along stand in the way of progress for their community. If the community cannot be unified around more good jobs, about what can it agree?

THE POPULIST CITY

Perhaps the opposite of the competitive city is the populist city.[3] It is best represented in most cities, including Springfield, by grassroots neighborhood leaders. Over the more than twenty years that I have served on the Springfield City Commission, we have experienced an explosion of neighborhood associations. Back in 1988, only four or five neighborhood associations were valiantly holding on against tough odds. They really were left over from the Model Cities days of the 1970s, when the city had several staff members whose jobs were to assist neighborhoods in getting organized. As federal funds were withdrawn and the city budget was cut back, this staff disappeared. With the support of the new commission elected in 1989 as neighborhood allies, neighborhood associations began to appear again. With a little city financial support and the addition of a neighborhood facilitator, many more associations emerged. Now there are around forty neighborhood associations officially recognized by the city.

Throughout this story of neighborhoods, one element has been consistent: a deep suspicion of the established powers in the city and a firm belief that the neighborhoods know best. Back in the Model Cities days, this divide led to constant battles between the city and the neighborhood groups. In the late 1970s and early 1980s, the conflict became focused in the battle mostly over whether federal funds should be spent on downtown or in the neighborhoods. The Springfield establishment led the effort to level and to rebuild downtown. Symbolically, the group leading downtown redevelopment (Core Renewal) met at the exclusive Springfield Country Club. The Chamber of Commerce strongly supported this effort.

Given the general decline in city services during these years, neighborhood advocates concluded that their neighborhoods were being sacrificed for the sake of the establishment's agenda. In fact, however, much of the funding for many of the downtown projects could not have been used for the neighborhoods, and city services would have declined with or without downtown redevelopment. However, about four blocks of downtown were cleared using mostly federal funds, primarily Community Development Block Grant (CDBG) money, which could have been spent in low-income neighborhoods. There was a trade-off.

One lightning rod in this general debate was city support for a new YMCA downtown. The Springfield Family Y needed a new facility. It could have moved to the more affluent Northside, where the majority of its potential paying membership lived. From the point of view of the establishment, this was a simple call; it was best for the city to keep the Y downtown, which justified putting city funds into the project. Neighborhood advocates, including those on the board that recommended how the federal funds involved should be spent, argued that the Y should pay its own way and that the federal funds should be spent in low-income neighborhoods instead. In the end, about two hundred thousand dollars of federal funds was spent on the new Y, and the Y agreed to provide free memberships for some low-income children in return. This step did not satisfy the neighborhood advocates.

When I joined the Springfield City Commission in 1988, the downtown hotel project was the lightning rod at the time. Again, the establishment put the project together, which included finding a group of local investors who were willing to put up a portion of the funds needed and a hotel firm willing to build and operate it. It also involved a major federal grant to finance a low-interest loan to the project from the city. None of this money could simply be applied to neighborhood problems. However, CDBG money was spent to purchase the site for the hotel and land around it for parking, and to pay to relocate people and businesses in those locations. This money could have been spent on the neighborhoods. The hotel project was unpopular in the neighborhoods in part because people thought it would fail and in part because neighborhood people resented the establishment using "neighborhood money" for a project developed in secret by the powers that be.

In recent years, the neighborhood associations have formed the Council of Neighborhood Associations (CONA), and one neighborhood leader began publishing a newsletter, *Neighborhood Voices*. Even a casual reading of *Neighborhood Voices* or a few visits to CONA or neighborhood association meetings show that suspicion of the establishment is alive and well. Most often this attitude comes out in criticism of city government and cynicism about the sincerity of city officials. However, it also applies to institutions considered part of the establishment, such as the Chamber of Commerce, Wittenberg University, the Turner Foundation, the Center City Association, or the Springfield Country Club. Neighborhood advocates consistently have argued that the neighborhoods themselves should decide their future and that the city should support the goals of the neighborhoods.

A good example of this approach was the discussion in 2004–5 of a railroad quiet zone. Trains still run through downtown Springfield and through about thirty crossings in the city. Because drivers often attempt to beat the trains, their engineers blow their whistles early and often as they pass through Springfield. This noise creates problems for the downtown hotel, downtown housing, plans for a new downtown hospital, and other downtown development. The whistles could be quieted if downtown crossings were designed to make it nearly impossible to go around the gates. Federal and state officials were willing to help finance the quiet zone if five or six crossings on the Westside were closed. The establishment (the Marriott, Turner Foundation, Center City Association, and downtown hospital advocates) favored the quiet zone. The West End Committee did not want its crossings closed. Safety studies might indicate that it was safer, but they did not want their neighborhood cut up or isolated. In support of the West End Committee, CONA joined in opposing the plan. Experienced neighborhood leaders provided an established channel through which neighborhood concerns could be organized and taken to city government.

This neighborhood populism assumes that creativity is most likely to arise from the grass roots and that the little people know the realities of their lives better than does the isolated establishment. Community advocates insist that representatives from the neighborhoods must be involved in deciding the future of Springfield. Even more directly, they want as many decisions as possible made at as local a level as possible. This approach allows different solutions for different problems. It lets different neighborhoods experiment with different approaches and learn from each other's successes and failures. In the process, local community leaders develop leadership skills, and residents develop a sense of participation in working on their own problems.

In recent years, the popular term for the guiding principle of this view of the city is "empowerment." This principle envisions a city that is a collection of neighborhoods all able to deal with their own problems or quite capable of forcing larger organizations, such as city government, to do what they want. People backing the idea of empowerment suspect that any attempt to do things on a large scale is vulnerable to control by those with the most power while ignoring the common people and their concerns. It stresses participation and control by those without much power so that they can become empowered. In practice, neighborhood activists often use a conflict strategy to get what they want, in part because they do not trust the system to produce for them unless they cause trouble.

THE PLURALIST CITY

One thing a new member of the Springfield City Commission learns very soon upon taking office is just how many people and groups about whom they never have known live in this city. A few elected officials come to office believing that they have a clear constituency who are their supporters and obvious opponents who are their enemies. Many elected officials try to please everyone all of the time, which requires learning to talk and act very carefully. People often call this talking "like a politician," which means trying not to say anything that would upset anyone and so saying nothing much. I have seen many a new city commissioner learn painfully that sooner or later they will have to take a position that does not please everyone. The vast majority of elected officials think they might want to get elected again. They may not try to please everyone, but most do try to please at least a majority. To add a little more advanced math to this political equation, a politician has to worry not just about what portion of the electorate holds a particular position, but also how strongly those people feel about that issue. For instance, 80 percent of the voters can believe one way but not care a lot, while 20 percent may believe the opposite but care very much. Three votes against strongly motivated minorities of 20 percent may mean that up to 60 percent of the voters will not vote for that politician next time.

Beneath these strategies for political survival lies the third of our four angles on the city, the pluralist city.[4] Most elected officials naturally seek a consensus that includes as many people as possible and excludes people only when absolutely necessary. This method of governing pushes politicians to the middle and trains them at least to give the impression that they are trying to take everyone's point of view seriously. For instance, candidates for president typically claim that they represent the moderate middle—unlike their opponent, who is on some fringe or the other. At the local level, this press to the middle is accentuated by the access that most citizens have to their representatives. Most people who run for local political office do so in part because they want to help make government work for its citizens. Ignoring the interests of people who can look you in the face and make their case is a hard task. Frustrated citizens can stop a city commissioner at the grocery store or come to city hall or even attend a city commission meeting. Every commissioner with whom I have served tried to respond to what citizens wanted.

Those who hold the pluralist view see a city as an equilibrium that seeks to balance the interests of all the various groups that make up a community. According to this view, a city is successful to the extent that all groups, especially those with organized power, are incorporated into the community. The sign of success is peace; happy citizens are quiet, and unhappy citizens make noise. If a pluralistic city is functioning well, much of the action occurs quietly. A neighborhood that wants a playground gets one, another neighborhood that fears crime gets additional police protection, the leader of an ethnic group is appointed to a city board, a labor union gets a contract it can live with, a business group gets a tax break it thinks it needs, or petitioners get their street repaired. The fact that these things all get done without any public notice just proves how well the system is working.

When the process becomes public, the goal is to balance it and to bring to the table as many of the groups as possible that compose the community. The hope is to produce a result acceptable to as many of the important groups as possible. A favorite public procedure for pluralists is a nonpartisan blue-ribbon committee composed of representatives from multiple interest groups. This is not a formula for imaginative or controversial policy. Indeed, it does not even produce consistent delivery of services, because the goal is to deliver what people want, which varies by who wants what and when. It often is easiest to figure out why something is happening by finding out who wants it.

During the early and mid-1980s, Springfield City Commission meetings were battle zones. Angry citizens, most holding some version of the populist view, attended regularly to object strongly to everything from charges of police brutality to the latest downtown project, from scandals in housing programs to the newest cut in services. Those people with influence in the city did not attend public meetings very often, but behind the scenes they were very critical of city government for a decline in services and an inability to produce enough support for downtown development or economic development deals. This sort of chaos clearly indicates a failure of pluralist politics, an inability to rally broad public support for city government. Over the past two decades, that broad public support has been rebuilt piece by piece by turning the streetlights on, fixing the streets, reducing crime, improving housing programs, and trying to respond to citizen complaints. Each of these steps appeals to different groups of people. The sum total is a pluralist success: broad public support for a system that is doing everyone some good.

The railroad corridor issue mentioned earlier is a good example of what a pluralist does when there is no way to make everyone happy. I urged the city engineer to go to a meeting of the West End Committee in the fall of 2004 to present the plans including the railroad crossing closings to that group before they became public or even were presented to the full city commission, and I went with him. The West End Committee still opposed the closings, but they could not claim that the city was trying to slip something past them. In my discussions with the city engineer, he suggested that perhaps one crossing could be pulled from the closing list without jeopardizing state and federal funding, so I urged the neighborhood organization not simply to oppose all the closings but also to prioritize the crossings in case we could keep one or more open. At the public hearing held by our regional transportation planning agency, opposition was angry and absolute from people not previously in the West End Committee. We urged them to channel their complaints, petitions, and ideas through their neighborhood organization. When the proposal came before the commission, the Marriott, Turner Foundation, Center City Association, and downtown hospital advocates were there to support it. The West End Committee, backed by leaders of other neighborhood associations recruited at the CONA meeting the night before, spoke against the proposal but without the anger of the earlier hearing. They also discussed the pros and cons of leaving various crossings open. The commission voted to close all but one of the proposed crossings and to seek to keep a pedestrian crossing at one of the others for children going back and forth to a local school. The neighborhood people were not happy, but they also were not as mad as they could have been without early notice and some compromise. This was the pluralist approach at work.

Pluralists recognize that those with more power or money get more out of the system than those with less. If you do not have money, one way to develop power is to get organized. Politicians are particularly attentive to groups that can produce or hold back votes. Pluralists counsel populist neighborhood advocates to get organized so they will be taken seriously. In doing so, pluralists are promising that the system will take seriously the interests of those who do get their acts together and include them in the equilibrium that is a well-functioning city. Many pluralists may even see it as an appropriate function of government or of a political leader to help unorganized interests get organized or to represent unorganized interests until they are organized. So the Springfield City Commission has provided assistance to the organizing of neighborhood associations.

The natural process of pluralism is moderate compromise among various groups and interests. In a sense, the pluralist leader is the point of interchange between all of the various interest groups. Her job is to incorporate as many interests as possible into the overall process, producing action that is widely supported because it does what most people want. In contemporary lingo, a leader who is good at this is a good process person; good process people make few people angry and build consensus. They drive goal-oriented people, like corporate CEOs, crazy because the pluralists seem more focused on process than results. CEOs measure themselves and others by results. Pluralism's basic principle is inclusion of as many people and groups as possible into a smoothly functioning system. It is much less concerned with abstract principles than with providing what people want, and much less guided by precedent than by public opinion. Those who see the competitive city find pluralism much too long on process; populists point out that the pluralists may claim to be neutral, but they serve those with power and influence much better than they do average folks. Both find the compromise at the heart of pluralism very frustrating.

THE PLANNED CITY

If the pluralists frustrate the competitors or populists, they are in a constant struggle with the planners over governmental policy. Consultants like David Rusk are common elements of the planning approach.[5] Certainly, the entire Rusk process is the best example of the planning angle in Springfield in recent years. These days, businesses, nonprofit organizations, and governmental bodies think they need to develop mission statements, shared values, and a strategic plan in order to do their work effectively. Some visits to Springfield by David Rusk and the Wittenberg urban studies analysis laid the groundwork for Rusk's speech and the focus groups that followed. In that speech, Rusk described three basic directions for action. First, he proposed that the city negotiate agreements with surrounding townships for win-win annexation, by which he meant annexation that did not require withdrawal from the affected township but did involve tax sharing. Second, he recommended a countywide comprehensive plan that addressed transportation and land use, including arrangements for utilities. Finally, Rusk advocated local support for changes in state law that would disperse low- and moderate-income housing and provide for farmland preservation.

After focus groups basically endorsed these three directions, the next day we had the equivalent of a strategic plan. The Springfield City Commission directed City Manager Kridler to negotiate win-win annexation with surrounding townships. The regional Transportation Coordinating Committee, Clark County, and Springfield entered into a joint process to develop a comprehensive plan for the entire county. Conversations were opened with local legislators about possible state legislation. Taken together, these efforts constitute a major effort to plan for the future of the area. These Rusk-inspired efforts combined with new zoning regulations, wellhead protection for city wells, and new brown-site regulations covering our old industrial sites to produce a planner's dream.

Government bureaucrats are surely the most consistent advocates of the planned city. However, residents of an older neighborhood in southeast Springfield with a body shop right in the middle of a residential area do not want to hear that it cannot be closed down because it was there before the zoning law existed; they want planning. Residents of the Eastside wanted the city to get a new Wal-Mart to locate on their side of town instead of all of the stores flocking to the northwest; they want planning. Many residents of the affluent Northside are not happy with the recent growth of fast-food restaurants in their part of town; they want planning. Residents of the Southside want to know when the city will build some nice new middle-income housing on their side of town; they want planning. Sooner or later, most of us want there to be a law against what we do not like or a policy in favor of what we do like.

Planning requires some procedure for deciding upon a plan for what should or should not happen and some capacity to provide incentives or to regulate behavior directly in line with the plan. A consulting firm was hired to develop the comprehensive plan for the regional Transportation Coordinating Committee, Clark County, and Springfield. The consultants began by establishing a committee of forty people from various groups and geographic areas to direct the process and by holding listening meetings at three locations around the county, where in small groups citizens proposed issues for the comprehensive plan. They also gathered data from various sources and organized the suggestions from the listening meetings. Subgroups took responsibility for various areas of the plan—traffic, land use, housing, and so on—and developed preliminary goals that were presented for comment at a second round of public meetings. The question then was just how specific these plans should become and whether the relevant legislative bodies, primarily the city and county commissions, would pass laws in line with the plan. In all, this process attempted to pick up elements of each of the other three angles in order to develop a plan that would gain community support.

A specific example might help. Would the plan call for requiring that all new development connect to public sewers? Much of the most dispersed housing was built on septic systems. Initially, this was cheaper, but eventually it often created serious public health problems that might require trying to run sewers to the houses, usually at county expense. For the city, cheaper housing on septic systems created two big problems. It allowed developers to escape the need for the city's sewer system and thus not annex this new housing to the city. Cheap housing outside the city also made it much more difficult to preserve or restore city neighborhoods. If this requirement was included in the plan, then it would be up to the county primarily to enforce it with developers, who would claim that it is unfair to owners of developable land that was distant from public sewers and home buyers who wanted to live in the country at reasonable prices.

Planners assume that the public good is more important than the personal interests of developers and home buyers. They do not believe that an unregulated market recognizes the public good without government intervention. They think that a community can develop plans that are legitimate expressions of that public good and that elected officials can enforce those plans. They are convinced that the end result will be a more efficient and fairer community.

CONCLUSION

When the plans get in the way of a business deal, competitors disagree; when the plans do not allow for what a neighborhood wants, the populists disagree; when the plans anger a significant constituency, the pluralists disagree. In each case, the disagreement is one of basic perspective as much as of the facts of any particular situation.

These basic perspectives carry within them fundamental assumptions about what the most important purposes of a city should be and about what process is appropriate for setting and carrying out those purposes. Advocates of a competitive city believe the essential base of a city is jobs; they want results, and they tend to think that centralized leadership gets results more quickly and efficiently. Advocates of the populist city believe that good neighborhoods make a good city and tend to think that a process that puts power in the hands of neighborhoods is best. Advocates of a pluralistic city believe that an equilibrium among the various interests makes the best city and tend to support a process where elected leaders balance interests effectively. Advocates of a planned city believe that policies informed by the common good produce the good city and tend to support a process in which experts gather information and opinions and then formulate intelligent policy based upon that planning process. In other words, at their cores, these angles on the city rest upon different views of what makes for a good city.

Views about what is good are ethical positions. Those seeking to consider the ethical dimension of public issues facing cities would do well to consider the assumptions of these four angles on the city in trying to figure out their own ethical position. In my role as mayor, I begin in the pluralist position—just like most politicians. When I joined the city commission, Springfield certainly needed an effective pluralist to bring together a city torn by a decade of angry strife. If I had failed to play the role of a pluralist, I would have failed the people who elected me. However, as a religious ethicist, my focus is upon the final causes that are at the core of the good plans. As a result, I am not a pure pluralist who makes all decisions on an ad hoc basis by choosing what will balance interests best. Rather, I typically ask what is most just, and I like to believe that I am willing to risk doing something a pure pluralist might not do because I think it is more just.

Something like these angles defines the ethical context within which I work. I believe that each of these angles has a grain of truth at its core. I hope that recognizing and appreciating that grain of truth in each of these various angles makes it possible for me to understand and respect the perspectives of different people and groups. That may label me an ethical pluralist as well as a political one. There is some truth to that, but not in any simple sense, as will become clearer. For me, views of the good are rooted in faith. By this, however, I do not mean that they are rooted in any particular theology or church. In fact, our faith may not even be clear enough to us to connect to either theology or religious institutions. Yet what we think is good (especially if we act upon it) is itself an expression of our deepest faith commitment. So just what do I mean by faith?

Chapter 5

Living a Faith of the Prodigal Son and Good Samaritan

In his reflections upon the love of God, James Luther Adams described his wide travels in Germany between the First and Second World Wars. Lutheranism was founded upon the belief that grace rather than works was central to salvation in the Christian faith. Adams tells of eating meals in German Lutheran homes in which the father was the master of the home who treated his wife in a way that seemed to Adams to be quite inconsistent with grace. On the other hand, Adams described other meals in the homes of Quakers, a tradition that does not stress theological concepts. Adams felt that those Quakers actually lived out grace in their family relations. He asks which of these homes practiced grace-filled faith.[1] For Adams, real ultimate concern is a lived reality, not a theological concept. This is what I mean by faith. We may say that we believe in justice, but the real question is whether we act justly.

PARABLES OF FAITH

If the real test of faith is acting justly, then parables may be better expressions of faith than theological concepts. At their best, parables are stories that carry in them the reality and complexity of lived faith better than the best theological concepts. If this is true, then two parables express the essential elements of my faith: the parable of the Prodigal Son and the parable of the Good Samaritan.

James Luther Adams has urged the centrality of the prodigal son as a description of God.[2] He tells of gaining this insight while viewing a woodcut of the forgiving father embracing the returning son. In short, the story is of a younger brother who becomes restless and asks his father for his inheritance. He takes off to a distant city where he wastes it all on riotous living. One day he wakes up among the hogs and says to himself that he would be better off as a servant of his father. He returns home a whipped man, but when his father learns that his son is coming home, the father throws a big welcome-back party. The good older son, who has stayed home and worked hard, resents his father's reception for his younger brother, but the father's love is boundless and forgiving. This, says Adams, is what we really need to know about God.

The God of some of the most theologically sophisticated churches of Springfield is not the warm and forgiving parent of that parable. Their God is often a distant, cold, judgmental God—more like the older brother in the parable. The best Mother's Day sermon I have ever heard was in a black Baptist church. The preacher said that God was like Mama greeting you at the door after a bad day at school, Mama smothering you in a big hug when no one else in the world seemed to love you, Mama offering you some brownies and milk and an ear, Mama letting you know that you will always be her child and can always come home. As he talked, I thought about my own mom and understood what he meant. I suppose American men are overly sentimental about their moms, especially in their traditional roles, but what a magnificent image of God! I have found that belief in theological concepts does not always correlate with lived faith in love of such a God.

The Good Samaritan has much to say about how we should live in relation to such a graceful God. When a smart young religious scholar asked Jesus the secret of eternal life, Jesus turned the question around and asked the scholar what he had learned. He answered that we are to love God and to love our neighbor. Trying to catch Jesus, he then asked Jesus just who counts as our neighbor. In response, Jesus told the story of a man who was robbed and beaten and left lying beside the road. A priest and a religious leader came by but quietly walked past on the other side of the road. A Samaritan, a member of a group looked down upon by Jews, came by and stopped and helped the man who had been robbed. Jesus then asked his questioner who he thought was neighbor to the man who was robbed. The young smart guy reluctantly answered that the Samaritan was.

Again, many of the churches of Springfield that feature a theology that would withstand the scrutiny of most PhDs in religion sit in comfort on Sunday morning at some considerable distance from their neighbors in need. They may even think about the needs of their neighbors and pray about them. What they do not do is dirty their hands by actually touching those neighbors in need. They certainly do not risk the comfort of material success to help those neighbors.

I recently thought about this while I sat through the dedication service for a magnificent new building for one of the most successful churches in town. I am sure that, for some, the grand music and pageantry were deeply moving. I am also sure that that church meets many of the real needs of most of its members. By contrast, the Baptist church to which we belong is struggling in part because of our location in the midst of need and in part because we continue to risk our future in order to serve that need. I confess that I went away from that dedication service a little smug about our own church's faithfulness.

After the school levy failed for the third time in November 2005, one of the African American Pentecostal pastors in Springfield called two other African American pastors to ask what the three of them could do. Adding to their sense of urgency was the fact that the new superintendent of schools was the first African American to hold that position. She had inherited a mess and a number of controversies from her predecessor and had been forced to cut the budget dramatically after each failed levy. Now people were beginning to blame her for the problems. The three pastors decided to organize a series of prayer meetings to support the levy, to put it in God's hands. That is how I found myself going forward to be anointed and prayed over and then returning to my seat to kneel on the floor with my head on my chair and pray for God's intervention in support of the school levy. None of this was typical of the worship to which I am accustomed, and the theology did not easily mesh with my process theology. However, these people prayed for the school levy while churches that worship my way and share more of my theological position did not. I say these African American ministers and I share a faith beyond worship style and theology.

So, I am at home among those who live a faith of the Prodigal Son and Good Samaritan, a faith in a graceful God lived in service to those in need, regardless of the theological concepts they use to describe that faith. Now I think that it is helpful to have a theology that is consistent with my faith, and for me that is process theology. I believe that it best expresses what a graceful God is in contemporary terms and helps me understand how to be a Good Samaritan in our complex society. I teach and write about process theology and believe it expresses my faith very well. However, I have found that when I suspend my judgment about the apparent theological content of the religious expression of a wide range of faithful people in Springfield and listen clearly, I often can hear echoes of the Prodigal Son and the Good Samaritan. I constantly am inspired and informed when that happens, regardless of style or theology.

BORN INTO A PUBLIC FAITH

I have never liked really hot weather, but there I sat in a hot little one-room Baptist church outside Hollandale, Mississippi, in June 1965 for their Wednesday night service. We sang songs of faith and courage and then heard young people testify. One after another, these young people spoke of their willingness to confront a racist system that had been more than willing to crush anyone who had challenged it in the past. I was convinced that these young people were truly willing to die for this faith, and they knew they might have to do so. Two days later, I sat in a much larger church in Jackson as we celebrated the court decision authorizing our demonstration against the state of Mississippi. We sang the same songs we had sung in Hollandale and others much better—but with no greater commitment. The speeches were much better—but not more heartfelt. I am in fact a born-again Christian, just not in the way that term commonly is used. I learned the faith of a loving God and service of others from my parents and my church, but I found God immediately present in the public struggle for justice in the civil rights movement. I was born again by that experience. That faith found in public life has been confirmed over and over in my public life since. That faith has inspired my political action for nearly two decades in Springfield, Ohio. I want to be crystal clear that this is not the application of the faith of my personal life to public life. Rather, it is the faith I continually find renewed by my experience of God right in my public life.

LIVING FAITH

This faith in justice arises out of both negative and positive realities. On the negative side, the social order we live in is not just. By social order I do not refer to some sociological concept but rather to the everyday world in which we live. We expect that our cities will be segregated by race and income and that jobs that are held mostly by women will pay less than jobs held mostly by men, that young people who attend suburban schools will be more likely to succeed in college than those who go to urban or rural schools. Why? We understand, whether we consciously admit it or not, that our society is organized that way. That is what I mean by social order. But it is not always negative. Some poor families support their children, some inner-city teachers educate their students, some city neighborhoods are safe, and some employers pay good wages for good work. The God who is love lures us to living personal lives of meaning and integrity and to creating a social order that is just.

The emphasis on justice always sounds like grit-your-teeth religion. Some of my public life is like that, but much of my experience in public life is much more joyful. I have found people of courage and wonderful spirit at work, trying to make our society more just. Time after time I see average citizens working long hours for no pay to organize a neighborhood association to make better the place where they live. They put up with people not showing up for meetings, with city officials who do not always seem to care, with disappointments as much as successes in order to realize the satisfaction that comes from working together on community issues. For more than two years, I met with elected officials from Clark County and Springfield Township to hammer out an agreement about how to pursue our future together. Along the way we reached more than one dead end, and all of us thought about giving up on the process more than once, but we did not do so. When we were done, we all felt the exhilaration that comes from feeling that together you have done something that will make the world better for years to come. In our own little way, we had made history together.

I do not mean to denigrate the value of individuals of deep personal religious faith. I have been loved and supported by them, and I humbly seek to live out my own faith in my personal relations. However, I have known the experience of the faith of public life too often to ignore its equal pull upon my heart. Justice achieved is always fragile, requiring continuous acts of faithful courage to sustain and expand itself, but it is a joy that rivals the joy of a personal faith well lived. My life as a member of the Springfield City Commission has been many things— important and trivial, generous and mean. One thing it has been for me is a place where I meet and seek to embody the love of God. For me, meeting and trying to embody the love of God in public life affects how I live my public life in two ways. It has implications for how I view policy options, and it gives me hope.

IMPLICATIONS FOR POLICY

I was checking out at a local hardware store the Saturday after a particularly difficult commission meeting when the store clerk said to me, "You are Warren Copeland, aren't you? I saw the meeting on TV. You always let people have their say. People appreciate that." I have learned that people want to be heard and want to be treated with respect, often more than they want to win the day. At times, they are unbalanced in their view of things, and sometimes they are insulting. But do not all of us deserve to appear in public and have our say? Is not this basic respect for the integrity of all people exactly what the founders of the United States declared was endowed in us by our creator? I believe so, and that belief is rooted in the God I experience in public life. Sometimes I fail to act on that belief, but I think it is fundamental.

Somewhere I read that how we treat "the least of these" is a primary test of our faith.[3] I believe that this concern for the disadvantaged is just as true of our public life as it is of our personal life. I always ask myself how my vote on an issue will affect those who have less. The answer is not always clear. Often those who advocate a tax break for a successful business claim it will create jobs for those who need it. Will it really? Annexation—which seems to have nothing to do with the least of these—helps provide the tax base that will help finance services for our low-income neighborhoods. I am not sure that I always get it right in practice, but I am convinced that I must always ask the question to the best of my ability if I am to be faithful to the God I experience in public life.

Most of the decisions that we make in local government do not involve complicated ideological positions. Rather, someone wants us to give them something at the expense of their fellow citizens. I have found that most of those who advocate free markets and limited government in every other case usually are willing to use the government when it helps them. Similarly, many are ready to redistribute everyone else's income to the poor but want to keep their own. Who will be committed to the good of the whole community in the face of the demands of self-interest from its members? I believe, as the elected representative of the entire community, that this is a central part of my job. This belief arises from my faith in the God I experience in public life. I seek to make my decisions as a public official guided by these three ethical principles: respect for the integrity of all people, concern for the disadvantaged, and commitment to the good of the whole community. Sometimes I think I succeed; sometimes I know I fail. I believe that all three are rooted in the grace of God received by the Prodigal Son and the love of neighbor acted out by the Good Samaritan. At least, that is my faith.

These three ways of viewing policy options help place me among the angles on the city described in the last chapter. The Prodigal Son returned home because he was broke. Jobs are key to a community. A mayor inspired by the father who welcomed his son home would seek to provide an economic home in the form of jobs for the city's citizens. The questions are to what extent a city should compromise its capacity to provide basic services to its citizens (many without a lot of resources) or undercut the quality of the entire community in order to get those jobs. The answers are probably not as much as chambers of commerce want. A mayor who respects every citizen and seeks to support underdogs has to feel real empathy for neighborhood groups fighting to be heard and to preserve the livability of their neighborhoods. Their limitation may be that they do not always see the big picture, the overall good of the community. However, they always have a right to be heard and must not be dismissed too easily just because people with more power want to do something that affects that neighborhood. The planners try to see the big picture. However, the planning process often is managed by experts and people with resources to hire experts to figure out how to use plans to accomplish their goals. A mayor looking out for the least of these or the public good must try to include the interests of those without the expertise or the money to buy it in the planning process and the functioning of the resulting plans. Like it or not, a mayor begins from the point of view of the pluralist. However, if all that a mayor tries to do is to keep peace and to keep as many people happy as possible, substance is replaced by process, and being in office loses its purpose. The mayor can become the modern-day equivalent of those who passed by on the other side of the road. This particular mayor promised himself that if that day came, he would find something else to do with his life.

HOPE

That leaves the problem of hope. Some days when my students start mouthing the cynical comments about politicians that have become commonplace, I stop the class. I tell them that the voters get much better politicians than they deserve. I tell them that every member of the Springfield City Commission with whom I have served—those I have agreed with and those I have disagreed with, those I have trusted and those who have lied to me—every one of them wanted the best for the city. As a group, they certainly were more respectful of human dignity, more concerned about those left behind, and more committed to the public interest than any group of typical citizens I know. We have been a motley crew, but not a selfish or insensitive one. I am much better for knowing them and working with them.

I have been married to the same woman for more than forty years and am proud of the lives we have made. Together we have raised two good children and now enjoy our grandchildren. We have been active members of churches our entire adult lives. We have tried to reach out directly to those persons we knew needed help and have been deeply moved by the love we have received back. I have taught thousands of young people how to think more deeply about critical issues in our society, and it is so gratifying to have former students tell you that you have made a difference in their lives. I have written books and articles beyond what is typical of a professor at a liberal arts college like Wittenberg, and I enjoy seeing myself quoted or having colleagues say they are using one of my books in a class. However, no experience I have had in life has given me more of a sense of making a positive contribution to the lives of others than my work on the Springfield City Commission.

God offers us no promise that our private or public efforts will succeed. In the struggle to realize love and justice in our personal and public lives we come to know the value of love and justice and to experience it in our very beings. I sense that I have been a part of a historical turn for the better in the story of Springfield, and that sense breeds hope. Regardless, I must testify to the fact that I have found public life an adventure I would not have missed. Along the way, I have found God calling me forth to the struggle for justice in the midst of that public life, and my faith has been challenged and renewed.

Chapter 6

Freedom and Diversity

Principles for Contemporary Cities

In *Adventures of Ideas*,[1] Alfred North Whitehead describes how ideas arise out of the lived experience of people and their societies. He then traces how one particular idea, freedom, developed over centuries until it inspired action to end slavery. Ideas arise from reality and then change history. Now there is a concept that might help make it seem less crazy for a college professor to be a city commissioner. Whitehead wrote *Adventures of Ideas* at a time when the central question for cities was whether and how industrial society could be brought under human control. In the United States in recent decades, we have added the question of whether and how sprawl can be brought under human control. I want to explore these questions and to propose that freedom and diversity are fundamental commitments that can inform our answers to them.

SPRAWL IN SPRINGFIELD

In the 1920s, residents of Springfield, Ohio, had bragged that Springfield was the best city of sixty thousand residents in the Western Hemisphere. By 1933, their enthusiasm was being tempered some by the Great Depression. However, they still assumed (usually without much reflection) that heavy industry was the fundamental base of their community. Springfield was a successful midwestern industrial city. It was just the sort of industrial city about which Whitehead wrote with real concern for the capacity of humans to bring it under some control.

The trend toward the dispersal of urban settlement that Whitehead saw getting started in 1933[2] has gained momentum with results that threaten American cities in the early part of the twenty-first century. This is nowhere clearer than in the Midwest, where cities like Detroit, St. Louis, and Cleveland are the terminal examples. Whether we call it suburbanization, sprawl, or expansion, the wealthier classes that Whitehead saw moving to the outskirts of cities prior to World War II were followed after that war by millions of people who are less wealthy. In search of better schools, less crime, more bathrooms, and bigger garages and yards or just distance from the people and problems they associate with the city, these people moved to new residential areas on the outskirts of cities. Shopping centers soon followed their customers to the suburbs and attracted even more people.

These residential changes have been compounded by changes in work. When I grew up in northwestern Illinois, most of my classmates went directly to work at John Deere or International Harvester making farm implements, some without even graduating from high school. Under a good United Auto Workers contract, they became solidly middle class and are now retired after more than thirty years of service. Their children cannot do the same thing. The number of well-paying factory jobs has declined dramatically; now most jobs that pay well require more education. Good schools are more important to the economic health of a community than ever before.

These changes in the nature of jobs have implications for location. Old factories were located around railroad tracks. In Springfield they spread along either side of the tracks mostly on the Eastside and Westside. Increasingly, good jobs are tied to telephone and computer lines rather than railroad tracks. It is more economically efficient to locate these jobs in the suburbs close to the best-educated workforce rather than in the city. Even most of those distribution jobs that require transportation are better located on the outskirts of town near the interstate highway than along the railroad tracks in town.

As I have already described, I grew up in an economically composite neighborhood in Silvis, Illinois. Mostly it was composed of the families of workers in the farm implement industry or for the Rock Island Lines railroad. There were some poor people in our neighborhood and some people on welfare. However, there were also Chappie Chapman, a vice president of the Silvis Bank, and Hap Weekley, a superintendent at the International Harvester combine plant. At times, Chappie helped those neighbors he knew could be trusted with loans; at times, Hap helped young people from the neighborhood land their first job. Silvis schools were not rich, but they educated most of us fairly well. The Silvis Park provided a safe place for me to play during the summer, supervised by high school kids. All in all, that neighborhood worked. The three-block area around my home may have been economically composite, but it was all white. However, descriptions of economically composite African American neighborhoods of the past have much in common with my old neighborhood. Middle- and working-class residents provided role models and contacts that were helpful to those less well off. They also made sure that neighborhood institutions like schools and parks worked fairly well. If anything, racial segregation forced working- and middle-class African Americans to stay in such economically composite neighborhoods longer than white people of the same income. Even with the enactment of open housing laws, working- and middle-class African Americans who do move out of high-poverty areas usually move into a somewhat higher-income area next door. All in all, racial segregation has changed very little in Springfield since 1960; the African American community has merely spread into adjoining neighborhoods.

As middle- and working-class families moved to the suburbs, many of these mixed, composite neighborhoods have disappeared. Most suburban subdivisions are homogeneous. Most of the houses look the same and cost about the same and thus attract people of about the same income. The resulting neighborhoods are not economically composite. In addition, the color line that has divided American cities now more frequently separates the mostly white suburbs from cities that are increasingly black and brown. In recent years, the color line also has jumped the city boundaries into suburban communities, creating nearly all-white suburbs and mostly black or brown suburbs. Our social divisions reinforce and are reinforced by political jurisdiction lines. When all of these people and jobs moved to the suburbs, they left behind urban neighborhoods in distress or in fear of deterioration. We have seen William Julius Wilson's analysis of the results. Neighborhoods that used to have some poor people now have mostly poor people because those who could afford to move out have. The concentration of poverty in these neighborhoods has been accompanied by higher crime rates, more single-parent families, and declining schools. According to the Wittenberg study, about half of the frequency of 911 calls for major crimes in Springfield are associated with the percentage of poor people in a neighborhood. That study also showed that test scores on state proficiency tests for fourth-graders vary directly with the percentage of low-income children in the school. Again, since Springfield has some primarily white neighborhoods where poverty is concentrated, these problems are clearly caused by that concentration of poverty—not by the race of the people who live in the neighborhoods.

As we have discussed already, Wilson argues that those who leave urban neighborhoods usually take with them role models, social support networks, and quality public institutions. The equivalents of Chappie Chapman and Hap Weekley of my old neighborhood move out, along with schoolteachers and well-paid factory workers. Stores close or become secondhand stores, churches leave, and schools and parks deteriorate. These neighborhoods are left not only financially poorer but also poorer in human supports and associations. Having seen deterioration up close, the people who live nearby are scared to death that their neighborhoods will be the next to go in the same direction. In Springfield, we have had an explosion in neighborhood organizations in recent years—mostly in neighborhoods on the edges of areas where the poor are concentrated. To some significant extent, these associations are fueled by quite reasonable fear.

As middle-income taxpayers moved to the suburbs, cities began to experience fiscal problems. When offices and factories followed, these problems became crises. No matter how competent city governments are, the underlying financial realities remain. They face all of the problems of a high concentration of people with greater needs—crime, older housing, streets and sewers that are wearing out—without the tax base to finance solutions to these problems. Failure to solve these problems or tax increases to try to do so merely lead more people and firms with resources to leave the cities for the suburbs.

The net result of this dominant urban dynamic is what I call the "daisy" American city – a concentrated and usually darker center surrounded by prettier and generally lighter petals. We have come to think of this as an inevitable and even natural development, thus the daisy image. This has become simply the way cities are, most dramatically in the older cities of the Northeast and Midwest, and this reality seems beyond human choice. This sense of the inevitability of sprawl for postindustrial American cities feels to us just like industrialization felt to our ancestors during the early years of the last century. The basic dynamics of industrialization also seemed powerful and even inevitable. Most of all, humans did not seem to have the capacity to make choices about what direction this industrialization should take. This sense of impotence is a major impediment to effective action for dealing with sprawl in our day.

WHITEHEAD'S ANALYSIS OF INDUSTRIAL SOCIETY

Industrial society offered a new way of providing for the most elementary needs of people. It promised to produce basic consumer goods with an efficiency that would make them available to the masses, but industrialization also dramatically undermined traditional ways of living.[3] In Springfield, factories literally tore up neighborhoods and planted massive new plants that dominated the landscape and dramatically changed the environment. These factories served as magnets drawing new transportation routes and other factories and workers who settled around them. At the same time, they dramatically changed our social and personal lives. Working in a factory was a very different experience and created very different family lives than working on a farm or in a small town. In time, the struggle for industrial unions and their subsequent success dramatically shaped the social and political life of Springfield and other industrial cities. Industrialization proved to be a much more dynamic force in our lives than anyone had predicted.

Many claimed that industrial development was too powerful to be denied. Public water and sewers, transportation, fire protection, and police power were all expected to serve industrial expansion. Failure to serve this development would merely cause it to go to some other city to work its productive wonders there. At various times, child labor, long hours, unsafe working conditions, environmental destruction, and especially management control over workers were defended as necessary to serve industrial development. Its advocates claimed that human concerns must give way to the demands of machines, and attempts to bring industry under human control were criticized for not accepting necessity. In the face of this relentless development, Whitehead argued for human agency.

Whitehead recognized that industrial development made it more possible to provide the necessities of life: food, warmth, and shelter.[4] Opponents of industrialization who ignored this positive contribution did so at the risk of either irrelevance or injustice. No doubt industry disturbed the comfortable and genteel life of the elite of the preindustrial age, but that was a small price to pay for its productivity for the masses. However, much that was justified as necessary to meeting basic needs was actually industrial owners using the power they had obtained to treat workers unfairly and to destroy nature unnecessarily. Finally, these advocates of industrialization argued that its demands were so necessary that political intervention was either futile or would get in the way of the good that industrialization was doing. They sought and received political support for industry's effort to control its workers and markets.

It is this attempt to exempt industrialization from human choice by seeing it as a natural necessity rather than primarily a human activity that Whitehead sought to undercut. Whitehead thought that by 1933 it was obvious that letting industry run free in the name of free-market capitalism had proved a failure. While he thought that the power of industrialization to meet basic needs was clear, he believed that the need to control its destructive capacity and to channel it to serve human purposes was obvious. This raised the question of what positive ideal could inspire and guide democratic control over this powerful dynamic force in human affairs. In this context, Whitehead proceeded to examine the place of freedom in human affairs.

WHITEHEAD ON FREEDOM

Whitehead decried the limited understanding of the idea of freedom held by the intellectuals of his day.[5] He thought that they too often confined the concept of freedom to freedom of thought, freedom of the press, and freedom of religious opinions. The limitations to freedom are conceived as wholly arising from the antagonisms of our fellow people. In our day we might call this the popular culture theory of freedom, the freedom to keep doing something ever more shocking. It has become the centerpiece of what has been called the culture wars. To the advocates of this understanding of freedom, even opposing violent pornography is censorship that no advocate of freedom should contemplate. To the contrary, Whitehead urged as follows:

> The essence of freedom is the practicability of purpose. Mankind has chiefly suffered from the frustration of its prevalent purposes, even such as belong

to the very definition of its species. The literary exposition of freedom deals mainly with the frills. The Greek myth was more to the point. Prometheus did not bring to mankind freedom of the press. He procured fire, which obediently to human purpose cooks and gives warmth. In fact freedom of action is a primary human need.[6]

For Whitehead, the central challenge of freedom in the face of industrialization was whether the capacity of reasonable persuasion in the form of democracy could expand to direct industrialization's power in more humane directions. Child labor laws, worker safety, union rights, antitrust laws, and environmental regulations are all aspects of this expansion of democracy into areas where industry once had its way unchallenged.

It may be obvious, but it is important to notice that real freedom not only allows us to shape reality but also provides a principle to guide our attempts to change the course of history. Democracy should direct industry toward allowing and even supporting wider opportunities for freedom. Freedom used well makes possible even more freedom. For instance, the central purpose of child labor laws is to expand the capacity of children to exercise even more freedom in their lives. More critically, it was appropriate to limit the freedom of the owners (e.g., to pollute the air) in order to increase the freedom of people affected (e.g., by what came out of the smokestacks). Freedom is both the principle of action and the purpose that action should serve, the basis of action and a standard of justice.

Whitehead's observations about industrialization and freedom are typical of his fundamental philosophical position.[7] Life is a dynamic process. All of reality, even that like industrialization that appears to be so automatic and overwhelming as to eliminate freedom, allows some element of choice. However, choices once made forever change the nature of the reality that is passed on to the future. For instance, the choice to have slavery in the United States changed the nature of the choices available to Americans ever since; it set in motion a string of choices that has dramatically shaped our contemporary cities. We can wish it had not happened and regret that it did, but that does not change the reality we inherit from the past. Every moment is significantly determined by the past out of which it comes, including the habits that clustered around industrialization. Contemporary analysts use the term "social structure" to refer to those accepted ways of doing things that we take so for granted that we often do not even notice them, even though they limit our freedom of choice dramatically. Freedom is never absolute. While ideals like freedom do not allow humans to escape the limitations the past presents us, they do lure us to more humane ways of shaping the future.

IMPLICATIONS OF SPRAWL

What is the relevance of Whitehead's discussion of industrialization and freedom to the realities of contemporary American cities? First, the struggle between industrialization and freedom continues as a primary theme in urban life, especially for cities that retain at least some industrial base. Springfield, Ohio, needs jobs. We try to keep our current employers and to attract businesses that bring new jobs. Businesses must decide where to locate. As they make that decision, one thing they ask of the city of Springfield is tax breaks. From their point of view, taxes are a cost of doing business; if their competitors get tax breaks and they do not, they will not be competitive. The situation often is stated very starkly. Without a tax break, they will locate somewhere else. From the point of view of the city of Springfield, there appears to be no real choice. Time after time, cities are asked to undercut essential services such as schools in order to serve the demands of industry. And it still is the case that choices could be made at the state and national levels to eliminate the competition between cities for tax breaks.

Added to this perennial struggle between industrialization and freedom is the overlapping struggle between sprawl and diversity. Surely the expansion of daisy cities often appears as automatic and necessary as industrialization seemed to many at the beginning of the twentieth century. Indeed, the fact that we usually call it "development" suggests that it is but a natural part of some maturation process. Sprawl's champions assume it is not to be denied and that anyone who tries to slow it down or divert it in more positive directions is standing in the way of progress. Like early industrialization, sprawl dominates and changes its environment with little regard for human consequences. It seems like a mindless natural process.

The critics of sprawl see it much more as a cancer growing out of control into the healthy countryside, threatening essential farmland and killing the cities' cores. Like the opponents of industrialization, these critics ignore the positive contributions of urban growth and romanticize the past. Most economists would suggest that increased productivity in farming simply makes farmland less valuable and its loss less of a problem. The old Eastside and Westside neighborhoods of Springfield built around the old factories belching the smoke of industrial America were far from ideal places to live. Not a week goes by that someone does not make a point of telling me that they grew up in one of those neighborhoods and are sad about its deterioration. They do not seem to recognize that folks like them who left helped speed that deterioration, but they did leave for what they considered good reasons. Similarly, most old Springfielders decry the loss of downtown and neighborhood stores. That does not keep them from shopping at malls and big-box stores. Suburbanites like their green space and attached garages. Most city dwellers would, too. The parking lot at Wal-Mart is full, and the new grocery stores offer luxuries to the average shopper that we never saw at the Tri City grocery store back in Silvis. Like industrialization, sprawl has served some basic human needs. Like opponents of industrialization, opponents of urban growth who ignore this do so at the risk of irrelevance or injustice.

However, as in the case of industrialization, sprawl has been facilitated by political decisions. As we have seen, economists use the term "filtering" to describe what happens when new housing is built and older houses are passed down usually to persons with less income. It sounds like a perfect market.

However, our urban daisies have not just sprung up naturally. They have been cultivated or at least fertilized by huge public investments that were the result of choices by human beings. The interstate highway system and especially the bypasses built around the edges of nearly every American city were essential to suburban development. Sewers and water systems, often built with support from state and federal governments, made sprawl possible. Low-interest mortgage money came with VA and FHA guarantees. Even the fact that homeowners could deduct mortgage interest on their federal income taxes encouraged the process. In recent years, various business tax breaks have helped the commercial and industrial firms to follow. At the end of the filtering process, a vacant structure must be rehabilitated or demolished. Often some public money is involved in either case. A similar process applies to commercial and industrial property. Urban decay is one of the costs of suburban development often borne by the public. Sprawl can be seen as the natural working of the market only by ignoring huge public subsidies at the beginning, middle, and end of the process.

Just as labor laws and antitrust legislation sought to direct industrialization in more humane directions, voices have appeared advocating democratic redirection of sprawl. Proposals include requiring that new suburban housing developments include low- and moderate-income housing, establishing boundaries around cities to force growth back into the city, and developing metropolitan systems for meeting needs and sharing tax resources. In order for such proposals to have any success in making our metropolitan areas more just, they must take account of the basic needs suburbs serve. They also must offer ways of addressing problems of the entire metropolitan area that the various jurisdictions cannot solve on their own. But what ideal would lure people to be an active part of a metropolitan area?

THE JOYS AND LIMITS OF DIVERSITY

Each fall Springfield, Ohio, holds a Culturefest. For one day, we gather and share music and food from the various groups in our community. Of course, here in the industrial heartland that features the African Americans and Appalachians who make up the largest groups that have not been homogenized into middle class Springfield. Bluegrass and gospel music share time on the stage with Greek dancers and increasingly with Latin music, and the smell of barbecue fills the air. In one tent, children listen to stories of the Shawnee Tribe that was here first. Irish music and German sausage remind participants of Springfield's largest European immigrant groups, and the tastes of Greek sweets speak of a later but significant addition to our community. Perhaps most interesting is that Culturefest has provided the occasion for the relatively recently arrived Muslim community of Springfield to appear in public. This celebration of diversity on the core block of Springfield brings together the sights and smells that those of us who love American cities treasure.

Especially during their preteen years, Ron Watford and our son Scott spent day after day together, unconcerned with their racial difference. Their failure to get much playing time on a summer recreation baseball team forced me into five years of coaching summer baseball. One year, our daughter Karen went to summer Girl Scout camp with Deanna Logan, an African American, and Justine Skelly, a blue-collar kid with Appalachian roots who was not sure that her mother's boyfriend was lying when he told her the girls would have to catch squirrels for food. Justine and Karen were justifiably outraged at the racist attitudes of some other campers toward Deanna. We envy our kids that their childhood friendships felt so natural, and we love our neighborhood for being a place where that could happen.

On the other hand, some census tracts just outside the city limits of Springfield are 100 percent white and have almost no low-income people in them. The schools that the children of those census tracts attend have almost no students who are not white or of middle-income. This is not an accident. Suburban subdivisions are designed to be homogenous. Most do not even have a very wide range of the middle class in them. They are built and marketed for a narrow wedge of the housing market. In Springfield those few middle-class African Americans who live in these neighborhoods generally have higher incomes than the average for the neighborhood. A former Wittenberg administrator once told me that what he liked about his neighborhood was that his children could associate with African American kids of their social class. Since most African Americans in Springfield cannot afford to live in these homogeneous upper-income neighborhoods, his children were not overwhelmed by African American friends.

Diversity is an ideal relevant to contemporary urban life, just as freedom was to the world of industrialization. Diversity does not, however, eliminate freedom as an important ideal. As we have seen, there is still a lot of industry around, cleaner though it may be. Moreover, the relative freedom that Whitehead described is essential to action in any arena. The residents of a neighborhood in decline worry a lot about crime and schools and boarded-up houses. But, as they try to get organized to do something about these problems, they discover an even deeper issue. Usually, most of the people in their neighborhood have given up, believing that nothing they do can change the inevitable decline. There are good reasons that they should feel that way; they are victims of changes in the nature of metropolitan areas that range far beyond their neighborhood and are driven by larger forces seemingly beyond their control. Practicability of purpose, the capacity to change the course of human events, remains a necessary reality too often in short supply in contemporary cities. Freedom and diversity must support one another if cities are to be good places for people to live. So what sort of ideal is diversity?

REAL DIVERSITY

Springfield's Culturefest and the friendships of our children are to full diversity what freedom of the press is to full freedom. Like freedom of the press, they are important, but they do not reach to the core of the meaning of diversity nor cut deeply enough to guide efforts to establish justice in our cities. Full diversity is not just difference; it involves three further elements.

First, real diversity requires individuals who have developed their own unique capacities as completely as possible. Working with neighborhood groups, I meet so many good and creative people who, like my own parents, did not graduate from high school. What greater contribution might they make to Springfield's diversity if they had the opportunities to develop their capacities like those of us who have been more fortunate? I literally am stretched further and thus have a richer life when I relate to others who are more interesting and capable. True individual freedom is not contradictory to diverse community; it is essential to it. And true diversity requires individuals who have been able to develop their uniqueness just as fully as possible.

Second, real diversity requires social justice. Many suburban residents serve as Big Brothers or Big Sisters to low-income children of single parents, trying to bring greater hope to those children. Often, they provide a valuable link to bigger opportunities, but what a Big Brother or Big Sister often learns is just how much the odds are stacked against their little sister or little brother. They often become discouraged about just how little difference they have been able to make in the lives of the children with whom they have been matched. At times, the children quite understandably come to see their Big Sister or Big Brother as a financial resource more than as a friend. The paternalism inevitable to relations between people with very different amounts of power makes true diversity very difficult. Diversity is not a substitute for social justice, and injustice makes true diversity impossible.

Third, real diversity requires interchange. A number of African Americans have crossed the color line in Springfield to live in mostly white neighborhoods, to work in mostly white places of employment, or to join mostly white organizations. When they do so, they know they will be judged by how well they fit into white ways of acting. A smaller number of Springfield whites have crossed the color line in the opposite direction to participate in things African American. While some may question their motivation, in my experience these whites experience much less pressure to act black. Similarly, low-income persons who participate in middle-class institutions generally are expected to act middle-class but not the reverse. We can distinguish between external relations, where we simply coexist with one another, and internal relations, in which we actually take into our own future the full experience of another. True diversity requires the interchange necessary to the development of internal relations. This does not mean that we become just like one another, the homogenization of the melting pot. It does mean that a part of who we are is our relationship to those very different from ourselves. In the process we become very different, more complex, and more interesting persons, and the community we share with those different from us is enriched.

In my discussion of faith, I described two fundamental faith commitments: Prodigal Son grace and Good Samaritan love of neighbor. Later, I also described three ethical principles to guide public action: respect for the integrity of all people, concern for the disadvantaged, and commitment to the good of the whole community. All mix some aspects of rational belief and essential insight; ethical principles are more rational beliefs and fundamental faith commitments are more essential insights. Where do freedom and diversity fit in this spectrum between fundamental faith and guiding ethical principles? I believe that they are closer to fundamental faith commitments. They can inspire beliefs about what is ethical, but like grace and love of neighbor, they are themselves more basic ways of living our lives.

We live in a society that is sprawling into suburbs that are marked by homogeneity; people of the same income and usually the same race are being sorted into subdivisions all over the United States. We celebrate diversity in word and popular media but not in living place. If real diversity is as fundamental as I have argued, this is a critical matter of faith and ethics in our society today. In spite of all of their problems, cities remain the center of diversity and offer that gift of diversity to the rest of America. Increasingly, that gift is less the real diversity I have described because it is marked by economic inequality that limits the development of its citizens. This leads to less and less honest interaction between residents of suburbs and residents of cities. Their worlds separate more and more. This distancing is compounded by an economy that is creating greater gaps between its well-educated mind workers and its less-educated body workers. In a vicious cycle, the gap between inner-city schools and suburban schools promises even greater inequalities in the future. I believe that this drive to homogeneous suburbs and the growing urban/suburban opportunity gap are fundamental issues of justice for the twenty-first century. These issues constitute the injustice we found in our study of Springfield, and commitment to real diversity is the needed theological response to it.

Articulating good principles is very rewarding for a college professor, but it means much less to average citizens. Only when those good principles become embodied in action through wise decisions can they take on the social reality that actually makes a difference in people's lives. For me it helps to make principles clear. Thankfully, many good people, as was true of my parents, can simply sense that embodying those principles is right and act on that good sense. Regardless, I am convinced that true diversity is essential to the future of cities. I also believe that true diversity, if achieved, can be the most profound gift of contemporary U.S. cities to humanity.

PART THREE
WHERE DO WE
GO FROM HERE?

Chapter 7

The Three *A*'s for Creating Diverse Cities

In the second part of this book, I identified the fundamental values of freedom and diversity and described the ethical principles of respect for the integrity of all people, concern for the disadvantaged, and commitment to a good community. However, as I described in the first part of this book, in the United States today most of us live in metropolitan areas that separate us increasingly into neighborhoods that are homogeneous and divided. In the process, our freedom to make our way in the world or even to choose a neighborhood that stands against these trends is increasingly limited, which is why I consider the shape of urban areas in the United States today and the trends for the future a profound issue of justice for our society. What might we do if we want to increase real freedom and real diversity in our metropolitan areas? In the third part of this book, I describe the kind of action we have undertaken in Springfield to answer these challenges. Again, I do this not so much to hold Springfield up as a model as to use our specific experience to illustrate clearly the difficulty of these challenges. Similarly difficult specifics exist in other cities across the country. Real diversity is essential for a contemporary American city if it is to survive as a viable human community. One key to that real diversity is breaking down the homogeneity of the suburbs. Another key is the retention of middle-class families inside the city and the attraction of new ones to the city. Otherwise central cities increasingly will become the home of only the predominantly nonwhite poor locked into neighborhoods that make it much more difficult for them to lead successful lives.

DISPERSING THE POOR: MPDU'S

When David Rusk visited Springfield, he told us of the housing policies in Montgomery County, Maryland,[1] and recommended that we urge the state of Ohio to adopt legislation that would enable similar policies here. He earlier had laid out a similar plan on a much larger scale for Baltimore, a metropolitan area that is very segregated by race and income.[2] (As far as I know, Baltimore has not acted on that recommendation in any significant way.) Montgomery County, Maryland, is not a typical county, let alone a city. It is one of the wealthiest suburban counties in the United States. Its typical resident is a well-paid federal employee often married to another well-paid federal employee. It roughly begins in Bethesda and extends outward to Rockville and beyond. Many of its residents are relatively well served by public transportation, primarily the Washington Metro, which carries them back and forth to offices in Washington. A majority of these residents believe government can effectively shape the private market for the better. They also are more committed to the value of relative diversity than most affluent suburban counties in America. Two sets of housing policies illustrate this, and Rusk believes they provide models for other metropolitan areas.

Most counties have a public housing authority that administers low-income public housing in its area. In the 1950s and 1960s, most of these local public housing agencies were building the housing projects we now have come to see as major social mistakes. These projects provided new housing far superior to the structures most of their residents had lived in before they were built. Federal regulations at that time required that every one in them be low income. This made sense if the goal was to help as many low-income people as possible; it did not make sense if the goal was to have neighborhoods that functioned well. Indeed, some of the project neighborhoods in Chicago were the very neighborhoods William Julius Wilson studied in developing his ideas about the human problems created by concentrating poverty. Montgomery County's public housing authority recognized the danger of projects early and decided to keep its public housing mixed in income. Since federal regulations did not provide for this, local financing through county bonds was used. They purchased some apartment buildings and converted some of the units to subsidized public housing but kept most of units as they were: rental units in the regular housing market. They built some new housing, but most of each of these complexes was market-rate housing. As a result, they did not end up with projects of all low-income people, and by all accounts they escaped the problems that accompany the concentration of poverty.

Rusk admires even more a housing program developed by Montgomery County itself that required developers to include Moderately Priced Dwelling

Units (MPDUs) in their subdivisions. Specifically, 15 percent of the units had to be made available at a price that was set by the county and adjusted for inflation periodically. The county further required that one-third of these MPDUs (5 percent of the total development) be made available to the public housing authority to purchase and use for low-income housing. Since the developers were going to make their money on selling the other 85 percent of the units, they had a strong interest in making the MPDUs look good and look similar to the rest of their units. In time, Montgomery County also required developers to integrate the MPDUs throughout the development rather than putting them all in one corner away from the rest. The goal of this program is to mix low- and moderate-income housing thoroughly into the suburban development. The theory was that this would create some diversity without producing the problems of concentrated poverty. It has meant that people with lower incomes than those typically locating in Montgomery County are now there, and many of them are not white. During the five-year period of 1992–1996, 41 percent of the MPDU buyers were white, 22 percent black, 28 percent Asian, and 7 percent Hispanic.[3] Rusk believes every metropolitan area in the United States should have such a program.

The Wittenberg urban studies faculty members who did the research for *Updating the Dream* accompanied city and county staff on a trip to Montgomery County organized by David Rusk to introduce us to these policies. We began with presentations by people involved in developing them, and then we boarded vans to see the results. We visited housing projects that mixed a majority of market-rate apartments with some low-income public housing units. They looked just like many other apartment buildings, clustered especially around Metro stops, that housed all of those Washington office workers. Then we went to some of the MPDU housing developments. In the same developments, we saw large homes even then selling for more than a million dollars mixed with smaller homes and some townhouse condominiums and apartments. All had similar design features. I could not distinguish between the market-rate and MPDU units. In one case, they were in the same buildings of about six units. The market-rate units on each end of the buildings had garages while the MPDU units in the middle of the buildings required parking outside. Otherwise they looked the same to me. Some of the MPDUs were low-income public housing. This diversity is limited and controlled, but it is much greater than happens in most suburban neighborhoods that developers build elsewhere. Whether with these policies or others, part of the diversification of metropolitan areas must include diversifying the suburbs.

That is a part of what Rusk calls the "outside game." The entire discussion of elasticity and my description of how we responded to the Rusk planning process were about this outside game. In Springfield, the CEDA agreement was a major part of this outside game. Most directly, it meant that the city would see its tax base rise as new development was annexed to the city. This is not what is happening to most of the cities in the United States, especially those in the Northeast

and Midwest. Instead, development is mostly on the edges of the cities in suburbs or unincorporated areas. The result is what Myron Orfield calls "the push
of concentrated needs and the pull of concentrated resources."[4] Cities lose tax
base while the percentage of poor people in their populations gets higher. This
produces fiscal stress that cannot be solved by good municipal management. The
CEDA agreement also creates the possibility of Springfield having more influence
over what happens on its edges through coordinated planning and zoning and
the opportunity to encourage more cooperation among school districts. I return
to that subject later. Efforts to create metropolitan responsibility, including funding for basic services, also is a part of the outside game. Springfield has pushed
for consolidation of public health, parks and recreation, public transportation,
emergency medical services, and public safety dispatching with some successes
and some failures. Rusk argues that without these changes in how metropolitan
areas operate—the outside game—it is hard for cities to preserve and to improve
the diversity and livability of its neighborhoods—the "inside game."

But cities also must play the inside game in order to create real diversity.
In *Inside Game/Outside Game*, Rusk summarizes a presentation by urban consultant Mark Bendick about retaining middle-class families inside the city and
attracting new ones to the city in the following terms:

> The key to success in luring middle-class families back to inner-city neighbor-
> hoods, I heard urban consultant Mark Bendick Jr. tell an Allentown, Penn-
> sylvania, audience, is to satisfy the three *A*s and the three *S*s. The three *A*s
> are ready *access* to high-quality job centers . . . ; high-quality *amenities* in the
> neighborhood . . . ; and high *affordability* of the redeveloped housing. . . .
>   Harder to satisfy—and much more critical—are . . . the three *S*s, begin-
> ning with adequate internal *space*. . . . Next are quality *schools*, the critical
> decision point for most middle-class families with children. . . . Last, and
> most important, is *safety*.[5]

In this chapter, I discuss the three *A*'s, using Springfield as an example. In
the next chapter, I discuss the more difficult topic of the three *S*'s, again using
Springfield as an example. The Springfield examples provide some concrete
material to illustrate the kind of problems that arise when cities try to address
these issues. Remember: other cities face the same challenges in somewhat different specific forms.

ACCESS TO GOOD JOBS

When suburbanization began in the United States, it was primarily residential.
The new suburbanite commuted back and forth to jobs that still were mostly
located in the cities. At first, even major shopping was still done downtown.
In time, small shopping centers and then larger shopping centers and then
regional malls and big-box stores located in the suburbs. Except for specialty
items, downtown shopping declined. Most downtown department stores closed

or lost business dramatically. Now city residents often must go to the suburbs to shop. Office and manufacturing jobs were much slower to move to the suburbs than was shopping, but move they did. Offices moved first because their people lived in the suburbs. As married women joined the workforce, suburban women provided a well-educated and very capable labor pool for the new office complexes that usually sprang up along major highways. Manufacturing was the last to go, and many of the dirtiest and lowest-paying manufacturers still remain. Those most dependent upon trucks to move materials and products, especially distribution centers, were drawn to suburban locations near major highways. Relatively clean and well-paying assembly jobs followed. For a time, corporate headquarters and financial institutions remained downtown, but many of them have also gone suburban in recent years. Some cities like New York and Washington have retained a large number of high-paying jobs downtown, but most now depend primarily upon public buildings, such as government buildings and medical buildings, and the professions connected to what happens in those public buildings, for such high-paying jobs.

As mentioned earlier, Springfield varied from this pattern of residential development. From the time Ridgewood was built in the 1930s and 1940s until the 1990s, it remained the neighborhood with the most upper-income housing in the Springfield area. Over time, other middle- and upper-income housing was added inside the city, mostly in the northeastern quadrant. Most of the new housing outside of the city before 1990 was primarily blue-collar tract housing. Even after 1990, expensive new housing was as likely to be built inside the city as outside of it. Most cities in the United States had expensive and exclusive suburbs long before Springfield did. (We return to this reality when we look at schools later.)

Commercial development in the Springfield area followed the national pattern much more closely. Neighborhood shopping centers often in the shape of an L came first. They often featured a grocery store or discount department store. If these neighborhood shopping centers began the decline of downtown shopping, then the Upper Valley Mall, located just outside of town, finished it. Now a regional mall in northwest suburban Dayton is the place to go for serious shopping for most Springfielders. This regional mall and the big-box stores located on the northwestern edge of the city in an area annexed to the city now endanger the future of the Upper Valley Mall.

International moved its assembly plant to the suburbs in the 1960s, leaving its stamping operation at the old city location until 2000. The primary location of new jobs (around sixteen hundred) from 1980 to 2000 was the PrimeOhio Industrial Park on the edge of town by the southeast outskirts, right near an Interstate 70 interchange. At present, Turner Foundation and the city are developing the Nextedge information technology park north of PrimeOhio in hopes of attracting five or six hundred jobs that pay well. By 2000, most of the good jobs left in the older parts of the city were directly or indirectly connected to government or the hospitals. This pattern is common in cities across the country.

During the 1970s, the Community Improvement Corporation tried to lure office jobs to downtown Springfield, including the national headquarters of International. The best they could do was Credit Life Insurance Company, whose business declined before it was sold and moved to Chicago in the late 1990s, leaving a nice, relatively new building. Core Renewal laid the groundwork for some great new buildings downtown in the time just before I joined the city commission, including a new city hall, a new jail, a new county building, a new Family Y, a new central library, a new hotel, and a new performing arts center. Later, the old city hall would become the Heritage Center, a museum of local history. All of this was important, but the Credit Life building remained the only significant new private for-profit investment downtown, and then the company collapsed, leaving the building. From time to time, restaurants and specialty stores opened, but most closed for lack of enough business to survive. In 1998, the Center City Association was formed to turn this situation around. With the help of the city and in time the Turner Foundation, Center City hired professional staff and developed some imaginative plans for revitalization. However, by 2000, it became clear that downtown Springfield stood in need of an infusion of well-paying jobs if it was to be able to support the housing, restaurants, and shopping that Center City envisioned.

A NEW DOWNTOWN HOSPITAL

Springfield had two hospitals for most of the twentieth century. One was City Hospital, owned and operated by the city until it became Community Hospital, a nonprofit operated by its own local board of directors. It has been located on its current site on Springfield's Eastside since 1932. The other was Mercy Hospital, founded in 1950 on the Northside and operated by the Sisters of Mercy directly and then through a not-for-profit corporation called Mercy Health Systems. More than once, the two hospitals discussed merging. In 1988 and again in 1993–94, they came close to that merger but could not come up with a way to handle women's health issues, most prominently tubal ligations, that was acceptable to the archbishop in Cincinnati. By 2002, it seemed clear that two hospitals could not both thrive and might not survive in Springfield. Lured by the dream of a single hospital with a state-of-the-art new building, merger discussions finally succeeded, and the new entity, Community Mercy Health Partners, was announced. It took another two years, until July 1, 2004, to negotiate and sign a final merger agreement. The archbishop approved an arrangement that would allow the Community Hospital Foundation to retain separate ownership of a women's health facility attached to the joint hospital. But where would the new hospital be located?

Groups committed to a downtown location for a new hospital began to push for that long before the new hospital organization was formed. The most obvious location was the area just west of downtown that featured a set of big old brick factory buildings used almost exclusively for low-cost storage. The Center City Association, with support from the Turner Foundation, looked for examples of downtown hospitals in cities like Springfield. They found one in Kalamazoo, Michigan, and sponsored a bus trip there to see what could be done. They then proceeded with plans of their own for the redevelopment of a corridor near the likely location of a downtown hospital. This corridor proposal featured green space surrounded by commercial and public buildings, including a new public indoor ice rink. This development would integrate well with the hospital development and indicated to the hospital that other sources of positive movement were taking place downtown.

The city itself proceeded on two parallel but connected paths. There was a proposal for a new cancer treatment center in Springfield that would bring together those involved in cancer treatment from the entire medical community of Springfield, including both hospitals. The city worked hard to see that center located near downtown. A location was found on the bank of Buck Creek, which meanders east to west through town just north of downtown. The site was home to an old factory building that was being used for storage and was just north of the location the city preferred for the new hospital. Working with representatives from both hospitals, city staff was able to find federal funds to demolish the building and clean up the site. The city commission had to approve moving forward before those federal funds were absolutely committed; the commission did so, and in time the federal money came. A beautiful new Springfield Oncology Center was built, featuring a chemotherapy room and a courtyard looking out on the creek. It was a magnificent addition to the community and very visible proof that the city and the hospitals, officially merged during the construction, could do great things together downtown.

At the same time, the city was trying to lay the groundwork for the new hospital itself. Using some of our economic development funds, we hired consultants to study traffic and architectural issues for a downtown site. This work and hours of additional effort by city staff meant that we were always able to provide numbers or alternative estimates through the entire process of choosing a location. Based upon these studies, the city actually purchased options on much of a four-block area that we thought was the best site for the hospital. An added bonus would be the removal of some ugly old factory buildings, including the old Crowell-Collier building. The traffic studies not only addressed access but also parking and the railroad. The possibility of a new hospital led to a new attempt to quiet the trains, producing the railroad corridor project discussed earlier. Another was the recognition that while a parking garage might be ideal, surface parking could serve the hospital adequately, at least in the short run. We also identified strengths of a downtown site, including its location in the center of our paramedic runs and access to complete and often redundant sources of utilities.

The merged hospital created a new governing board—half from the old Community Hospital board and half from the old Mercy Hospital board. The CEO of Community retired, and the CEO of Mercy became the CEO of the new merged hospital. At first the CEO chose to guide the selection process with a Dayton-based development firm that also wanted to be the developer for the new hospital itself. That looked like a conflict of interest to many, apparently including some members of the hospital board. In time, a local site selection committee was appointed, and an outside consulting firm was hired to assist with the selection process. A number of indications arose that both the CEO and the outside consulting firm preferred a suburban site, and they seemed to focus on one southwest of Springfield near the intersection of State Route 68 and Interstate 70. There was a growing sense that the decision was going to be made at the Cincinnati headquarters of Mercy Health Partners, which was taking the lead in financing the project. Almost all the locals I talked with were convinced that the decision already had been made and that the location would be suburban.

Then a miracle of public involvement occurred. A local group of citizens formed to advocate for a downtown hospital. They were led by a co-owner of a downtown auto dealership, a local builder, and the executive director of a job training center. HD (Hospital Downtown) buttons and a huge newspaper spread with pictures and quotes of hundreds of supporters of a downtown hospital appeared. The group met with the hospital CEO to urge a downtown location and to suggest that local support, including financial support, for a suburban hospital would be hard to find. The hospital announced forums to provide an opportunity for the public to express themselves. These forums were designed by the consultants to explain why a suburban location would be best and to limit response to filling out individual forms. The proponents of a downtown hospital turned out their people, especially at the last forum, to advocate for the downtown. "Hospital Downtown" yard signs went up all around town, and fliers appeared, announcing a rally at city hall, featuring city, county, state, and federal elected officials.

Behind the scenes, regular—usually weekly—meetings between city staff and hospital staff and consultants began. I participated a couple of times. In each case, I attempted to suggest, but not threaten directly, that the city was not likely to provide water and sewer service to a suburban site. Since the city was the only source of water and sewer utilities near the city, this suggestion would eliminate most of the suburban sites if we followed through. The hospital representatives, especially the consultants, were very difficult to move off of a suburban location. Their arguments were the same ones we heard from commercial clients. A suburban site was easy to develop and, if located near good highway access, would be easy to use. Over time, the conversations at these meetings became more candid and at times angry. The hospital CEO began to make the point over and over again in public that the hospital was meeting regularly with the city. We feared he was trying to lay the groundwork for choosing a suburban site, because the numbers would not work no matter how hard the hospital and the city tried. However, in every direction he turned, politicians, foundations, business leaders, and most of the public were united behind a downtown site. David Hobson, our member of Congress who was in a position to be very helpful with funding, made clear that he strongly supported a downtown hospital and was absolutely opposed to a suburban site.

Finally, the community pressure and the numbers began to have an effect on the site selection committee and the hospital board. Matt Kridler and his staff had developed cost estimates more solidly based than those of the consultants. They also met with state and federal officials to identify ways to finance a downtown location. All of these numbers convinced the hospital site selection committee that a downtown location was financially feasible. That is what they recommended, and that recommendation was announced in a press release two days before the city hall rally. This was a great victory for the community; we had stuck together and won out over the outside consultants. All such victories come at a cost. In this case, the first cost was a lot of public money (a total of $40 million) that could be spent on something else. But there was another cost that the city had helped create. Remember that pretty view of Buck Creek from the chemotherapy room of the new cancer treatment center? The hospital did, and they decided they wanted the same view for their facility. They chose a site on the creek bank north of the location that the city preferred, a site requiring the relocation of two or three hundred households.

At the urging of the hospital board of directors, a mediator was hired to work out the differences between the hospital and the city, and the hospital board directed their CEO to participate in that process. The same mediator had come in to bridge the differences between Mercy and Community hospitals, so he knew the players and problems. Through some hard negotiating, an agreement was reached. I had not been involved in the negotiating, but I was front and center for the news conference and public signing. Even before the agreement was signed, the city staff had laid the groundwork for state and federal funding. With the help of U.S. Representative Dave Hobson and Senator Mike DeWine, we received major help from the federal government. Our state legislators were able to help us secure a long-term state loan. Very little local money was necessary. The process of buying up property began in earnest, and the project moved forward toward a 2012 opening of a new $300 million hospital near downtown Springfield. As a part of the agreement, the hospital, the city, and two local foundations agreed to create a fund to acquire other property around the hospital site for other medical and commercial buildings. Nothing this important comes easily, and there remain challenges to face before the downtown hospital is a reality. However, it looks like it is going to happen.

Access to good jobs is the basic goal of those who advocate the competitive angle on the city. This concrete experience illustrates the challenges this approach faces when put into action, which means, in part, recognizing the interplay of this angle with the other three. In this case, the closing of the railroad crossings to facilitate the hospital development downtown in the face of neighborhood opposition was a victory of the competitive angle over the populist angle. That the neighborhood was involved fully in the decision and that some compromise occurred indicate some recognition of the validity of the populist angle. It is also a very good example of effective pluralists at work. The neighborhood was included, and some compromising was done. Hopefully, the neighborhood did not go away too angry, appreciating at least that they were taken into account. It was considerably more difficult to deal fairly with the people who lived in the area where the hospital chose to locate—in part because they were not organized and thus were not able to negotiate as a group, and in part because in some cases even a fair price could not compensate fully for the loss of a home. The city administration did hold meetings with neighborhood residents to explain the process and to inform people of their relocation rights. Planners were the clearest advocates of a downtown location as part of a comprehensive downtown plan. In fact, the CEO of the hospital and his consultants attempted to make a business (competitive) argument for a suburban location. However, the community rallied around the planners' view that a downtown hospital could restart the heart of the city. As mayor, I must be a pluralist much of the time, but I try to balance these various angles in a way that I believe will produce positive results for the community while creating more justice. This was an easy ethical call for me. The problems were primarily how to convince the hospital to locate downtown, how to force the hospital to pay its fair share of the cost, how to find the necessary public money, and how to minimize the negative impact upon those people who found themselves living in the way. Did my former colleagues feel the same about the downtown hotel that I had voted against when I first joined the city commission?

GRASS, ICE, AND WATER ARE AMENITIES

We sat at a table in a resort in Florida where we had come to plan the future of Springfield. Most of those present were members of the board of the Chamber of Commerce, but others of us were included so that the result could be called the product of an inclusive process. The question before us was what it would take to get CEOs of local companies to live in town. Across from me sat the Speedway/Super America group, including three current executives, and Dick Kuss, their former CEO. Raised in Springfield, Dick Kuss had done more than any other local citizen to make Springfield a place where his successors would choose to live. However, Dick's successor had moved the company headquarters to a site on the interstate outside of Springfield. Most of their current leaders now lived in suburban Dayton. When asked directly, the CEO discussed the quality of life in Beavercreek, his Dayton suburb of choice. I imagined that I could see a look of sadness on Dick Kuss's face; perhaps I was just feeling sad for him. Finally, Jim Lagos, a patron of the arts in Springfield, had had enough. "Beavercreek is a cultural wasteland," he said. "Springfield has an art museum, a symphony, a magnificent performing arts center, and great summer arts festival, just to name a few."

In fact, Dick Kuss had spent a lot of energy and not a small amount of his and his wife's money trying to create first-rate amenities in Springfield. When I came to Springfield, city government and Core Renewal were just completing the leveling of old abandoned downtown buildings and replacing them with a number of new buildings downtown. Dick Kuss was at the center of that process but not out front; that was Tom Loftus's job. A few years later the same people spearheaded the conversion of the old city hall into the Heritage Center, a museum that preserved and celebrated Springfield's past. Before that project was fully completed, Dick and Tom were back pushing improvements in parks and recreation facilities. As a result, a new aquatic center has been built and an indoor ice rink is planned, and older facilities such as Municipal Stadium (baseball) have been renovated. In each case, the formula was the same. Dick and Tom convinced private contributors of the value of the project and then approached public officials with the promise of significant private funding if the elected officials would find some public funds for the project. In the case of the performing arts center, that was primarily state of Ohio money funneled through the local community college. In the case of the Heritage Center, that was primarily Clark County money through a temporary sales tax increase that did not require a vote of the people. For the parks and recreation program, that was primarily city money and county money from a similar temporary sales tax. The end result has been the addition of a significant range of public amenities intended to be attractive to middle- and upper-income residents of Springfield.

In each case, the drivers of these projects are closest to the competitive city view of Springfield. They are trying to make Springfield competitive, especially for the upwardly mobile younger people important to the economic transition that Springfield must make from being a factory town to having a mixed economy. Perhaps at least some of those people employed in our new information technology park would want to live in a city with these amenities. Most of these projects meet basic goals of planners or flow from comprehensive planning processes, so they usually meet planning goals. At times, they do conflict with other goals, usually dealing with more basic needs, especially simple things like streets. If nothing else, they are part of the goal of diversifying our population. It is the populists who often have doubted the value of these amenities, especially compared to basic services to their neighborhoods. Does Springfield really need an ice rink? Just how many of our kids are interested in hockey anyway? That money could be used to build or restore a park in our neighborhood. Especially in a city like Springfield with people and neighborhoods under real stress, more immediate needs seem more pressing. The pluralists like city commissioners often feel the pressure from the populists and the legitimacy of many of their concerns. After all, I came to the office of mayor as part of a neighborhood revolution that saw Core Renewal as an enemy and with a pledge to restore basic services. However, populists want a viable city, too, and they often enjoy the end result. Country music shows are the only guaranteed sellouts at the Kuss

Auditorium, and one vocal critic of the sales tax for the Heritage Center is now a leading volunteer in their genealogy office.

However, we pluralists have to be careful. I attended a small ceremony to recognize a couple of our utility workers who literally saved the life of a fellow employee. As one of them sat down with the wooden plaque I presented to him, one of the other workers said to him, "At least it could have been in granite." Tom Loftus and Dick Kuss now have been joined by the Turner Foundation in the promotion of amenities. The Turner Foundation has a very strong commitment to doing things right and with a flair for design, which has produced some design statements that will leave their marks on Springfield for years to come. For some time, the Center City Association had sought a streetscape statement for downtown Springfield. The city had set aside some money that we would typically spend on streetlights and street repair as our share of the project. With Turner funds, the project became possible for the core block, but with some significant design upgrades. Most obviously, they added granite curbs to the project, an attractive but expensive addition. Various citizens began to ask why the city was putting in granite curbs while we are leaving other important needs unmet. This sounds very familiar to me. This is where I came into city government. I immediately tried to make clear that no tax money was being used for those curbs while trying not to seem ungrateful for this contribution to the city by the Turner Foundation. Such is the balancing act essential to the effective pluralist.

TOO AFFORDABLE?

Can there be such a thing as housing that is too affordable? Jeff Ankrom, the Wittenberg economist who is on our urban studies team, led a study of housing in Springfield that was submitted in August 2002.[6] One of its conclusions was that housing in Springfield was affordable, by which he meant that most people could find housing to rent or buy in Springfield for 36 percent or less of their income (36 percent is the level above which Fannie Mae, a primary government-financed mortgage lender, does not believe it should lend to home buyers). The fact that most people can find housing at or below the affordability level is not because income is relatively high in Springfield; it is because housing is quite cheap here. This is true for most cities, especially older cities in the East and Midwest. This is good news if you do not have very much money and you need a place to live; it is bad news for most older urban neighborhoods. When owners of property try to borrow money for major repairs to older homes or for building new homes in these older neighborhoods, they are likely to meet an appraiser. An appraiser estimates what a house is worth. Primarily, this is a question of what it might sell for in its location and condition. One thing the appraiser does is to check what comparable houses in the same area have sold for recently. If houses in the surrounding area have sold at relatively low prices, then that will reduce the appraised value upon which a mortgage would be based. The appraisal also is supposed to indicate the price for which a homeowner might be able to sell the house in the future.

The housing study of Springfield suggested that houses probably could not be built new in most of our older neighborhoods without government subsidies. There simply are too many older homes available in these neighborhoods at prices so much lower than what it costs to build new houses. Similarly, major rehabilitation of older housing in these neighborhoods probably would cost more than appraisals would justify without government subsidies. The exceptions would be homes of unique value like some of our old mansions or in neighborhoods where the entire neighborhood is simultaneously experiencing increasing housing values. This situation confronts urban planners and politicians with a difficult choice. In order to stimulate private investment in older neighborhoods, housing prices and thus appraisals must go up above the level that many of those currently living in those neighborhoods can afford. In other words, the most likely way to improve the housing in a neighborhood significantly is to replace low-income people with middle- and upper-income people. The alternative is government subsidies.

America's experience with subsidized housing is problematic. On the positive side, we have made it possible for many people to have shelter who could not afford adequate shelter otherwise. But in the process we often have created projects that have concentrated poverty with all of the negative consequences that Wilson describes so powerfully. As a result, most urban experts now agree that projects are a bad idea, and there is little government money available for them. The primary alternative has been rent vouchers through Section 8, named for a section of the Federal Housing Act. However, limits on the value of the voucher lead to the concentration of voucher recipients in lower-income neighborhoods. For example, for his housing study of Springfield, Jeff Ankrom mapped Section 8 recipients and families approved for Section 8 but waiting for the housing authority to have a voucher actually available. He found that the recipients are concentrated in low-income neighborhoods much more than those on the waiting list. Section 8 concentrates poverty, but Section 8 recipients are still less concentrated than those living in units actually owned by the housing authority.

One small solution to this problem is HOPE VI. It is one program financed by the federal Department of Housing and Urban Development (HUD) that funds local proposals that seek to disperse poverty, especially concentrated poverty associated with old public housing projects. The Springfield Metropolitan Housing Authority submitted a HOPE VI proposal that arose out of a lot of local consultation and some serious negotiation. It calls for demolition of 210 old units in the largest project in Clark County. In their place are to be built 108 mostly single-family public housing units, mixed with 38 single-family houses sold on the private housing market, but probably with some incentives such as down payment assistance and lower interest rates. Our nonprofit housing development corporation, Springfield Neighborhood Partnership, is formulating a similar program near the HOPE VI location that would feature even more home ownership. Hopefully, this action will stimulate current homeowners to invest in their own homes and even attract some private investment in new homes in the area. In turn, this might even lead Kroger to upgrade its grocery store that serves that area and the neighborhood where we live. In turn, we hope this might speed up improvements along the entire Limestone Street corridor—the southern entrance into the city that passes through some of our low-income neighborhoods.

Neighborhood Housing Partnership, a nonprofit housing development corporation that the city helped start in 2002, has also enjoyed important support from the Turner Foundation. It is in the process of beginning its Clifton Court project a bit north of the HOPE VI project. Located across from South High School in the Selma Road neighborhood, this project calls for fourteen new homes. This neighborhood is in our lowest-income census tract and has experienced the largest loss of people and structures in recent years. The builders association will build the homes to be occupied by homeowners. Depending on their income, NHP will provide some down payment assistance and some reduction in mortgage payments. Still, this is an attempt to change that neighborhood by attracting homeowners of more means than is now typical of that area. As with HOPE VI, the goal is to stimulate further development aimed at changing the neighborhood for the better even more.

These are our best current efforts to create affordability with livability. Good people are working hard with some resources to produce this result. They do not lack either imagination or commitment. However, it seems clear that this development will happen only with government participation. The private housing industry prefers building subdivisions in the countryside, and Springfield is surrounded by countryside. While our county land-use plan calls for limiting suburban growth and channeling it into areas that can be easily served by public utilities, public bodies have a hard time saying no to lots out in the countryside. Both appointed planning boards and elected officials continue to approve suburban sprawl. The valiant efforts to revive neighborhoods in Springfield described above and similar efforts in other cities all over the United States are fighting against what until now has seemed to be an overwhelming drive to the suburbs plus a now deeply troubled housing market.

Many of the neighborhood populists are discouraged by the constant decline they see about them in most older city neighborhoods. They rightfully are alarmed and often impatient with public officials who do not seem to be able to turn these forces around. Most advocates of the competitive view of the city see suburban sprawl as development in response to market demand. They insist that cities simply must make their neighborhoods competitive or lose. This healthy respect for market choices is a caution to those planners who think that reversing the suburban trend will be easy or cheap. Planners spin out plans, most of which gather dust. Those that are built generally are some cheaper version of the original plan that have less positive effect upon the surrounding neighborhood than was hoped. Pluralist politicians must support the neighborhood revitalization efforts but usually compromise with the competitive force of suburban development. I personally am convinced by the arguments of planners like David Rusk. As he puts it, the inside game of saving urban neighborhoods can only work if the outside game of limiting suburban development is won.[7] We have not yet won the outside game for housing here in Springfield or around the United States, but we continue the hard work of the inside game.

I can make my argument for diversity as a moral goal and for cities as the place to live out that goal, but the competitive city people are at least partially right. Real people who are a mixture of ethical sensibility and self-interest must believe that they can experience diversity without significantly compromising their interests and those of their families. Trying to address the three *A*'s is a part of that practical argument for the ethical good. While there may be some moral heroes who will sacrifice their interests and those of their families to seek diversity, there are not enough to preserve and extend the diversity that is the special gift of cities to American life. Like Springfield, all American cities must continually work to provide access to good jobs, increase high-quality amenities, and preserve the affordability of good housing if we are to keep and attract people who can afford to live in the suburbs. Otherwise, our cities will become homes only to those who cannot afford to live elsewhere, a few saints of diversity, and probably a few people of means living in guarded communities. That is not a real functioning diversity.

Chapter 8

The Three *S*'s for Preserving Diverse Cities

Actually the three *A*'s—access to good jobs, high-quality amenities, and affordability of housing—are the relatively easy ones. Jobs are key. We need all that we can find, and we particularly need to develop and keep a workforce with the skills that will attract jobs that pay better. However, most people know this is very important and have a pretty good idea of what it will take to get there. I can discuss what we are doing and need to do in this area to an audience and see heads shaking yes and get good questions at the end of my comments. While people may have questions about particulars, most believe the city should do what it must to bring the hospital downtown. We have found both private and public financial support in our community for improvements in public amenities as long as they are not too extravagant. They are simple and direct projects that produce visible results. Finally, while housing prices here are low, there is broad support for building new housing as long as it is subsidized by the federal government, not local taxes. The three *S*'s (adequate space, good schools, and safety) are much tougher.

THE FIRST *S*: SPACE

Of the three, space is less important to Springfield. Springfield never had a very concentrated population. If what people mean by space is something like our four-bedroom home, we have plenty of old homes of that size in Springfield. Indeed, the Turner Foundation has rehabilitated a number of much larger old mansions built during Springfield's glory days. If they mean bigger and newer, we have the housing built in the last fifty years, much of it just as large and with more bathrooms and garage space. Finally, if they mean new mansions that are both spacious and well located, we have a new neighborhood like that, too. The availability of all of these homes is partially a function of never having the kind of density of population true of larger cities. Springfield's housing has always been mostly single-family homes or duplexes; we have relatively few apartment complexes. More recently, it also is a function of little growth in population in the Midwest, and especially in Ohio. Add the home building that has resulted from low interest rates over the last few years, and we have plenty of homes with quite a bit of space. Of course, this does not mean that these houses are located where people prefer or in the condition they want, but that usually relates to the other two *S*'s: safety and schools.

THE SECOND *S*: SAFETY

When we balanced the budget for the city of Springfield in 1989, more of the 41 positions cut came from the police department than from any other part of city government. The reason was simple. The voters had established a minimum staffing level of 127 firefighters through a referendum that amended the city charter. Police made up such a large portion of what could be cut that even though their budget was cut by a smaller percentage, their personnel loses were the largest in pure numbers. The net result was that the number of police officers available fell as low as 89 authorized positions.

At the same time, the fastest-growing business in the older neighborhoods of Springfield and other American cities in 1988 and 1989 was the distribution of crack cocaine. Crack was a personal disaster for too many of our citizens. As I drove home at night in the dead of winter through impoverished near-Southside neighborhoods, I would see gray figures on corners in the freezing cold looking for a sale. I knew that they were on those corners in the dead of winter because they had to support their own drug habit. Addiction to crack had to be powerful to produce such motivation. Nevertheless, crack was a safety issue much more because of the violence that accompanied it. Unlike previous drug trafficking, the crack business was quite decentralized, and most of the dealers were very young. This made it much harder to control and produced much more violence when business was threatened or deals went bad. For the average resident of a neighborhood where crack was being sold on their street, it became a more dangerous place to live.

Politicians at the state and federal levels responded to the violence by passing legislation that increased the sentences for drug offenses, especially repeat offenses. Local officials also sought to respond, but knowing how was more difficult than neighborhoods thought it should be. The neighbors saw cars stop and deals made and could not understand why the police could not do something. If the police swept through a neighborhood and arrested everyone on the corners, they were usually back on the street within months or days or sometimes hours. Prosecutors said they could not make drug trafficking stick without a number of undercover buys by police. Otherwise, the charge was possession, and that carried lesser penalties. Undercover work usually took more time than the neighbors wanted. Success was measured in the number of dealers sent to prison for a significant amount of time.

Critics argue that the net effect is a serious problem not only for the individuals who serve time. Nearly all of them return to the very neighborhoods where they often are soon back in trouble. If they are unable to get jobs, they become threats to the neighborhood once again. Since the young men involved are almost all poor and disproportionately African American, critics say that in the final analysis we are punishing these young men for being born poor and/ or black. Clearly it would be better if young people never got addicted to crack cocaine. I am convinced that those without hope are much more susceptible to addiction, that economically depressed neighborhoods limit hope, and that race still factors into hope and economic disadvantage in our society and especially in our cities. None of this is very persuasive to those people who live in neighborhoods where there is drug trafficking. Income and race do not make any difference in their attitudes. I have never had anyone living in neighborhoods where there was crack selling complain that the police were doing too much. I have had a number of people from such neighborhoods complain that our police were not doing enough because we cared more about the more affluent neighborhoods than about theirs. In fact, we had much more police time committed to the neighborhoods with drug activity, but the people in those neighborhoods did not want to hear it. They wanted their neighborhoods back!

MORE POLICE

So, what could we do with police? The two directions that we moved involved the number of police and how they did their work. With fewer than 90 officers, the Springfield Police Department could not meet the crack challenge effectively. We simply had to have more officers. Recognizing this, the city commission asked the voters to approve a property tax levy to support additional police. We underestimated the residual lack of trust that was abroad in the public in 1989; that levy failed. Reasons given for its failure included that it was proposed by the city, that it did not guarantee a certain level of staffing, and that it included a little money for the rest of city government to pay for supporting the additional officers.

An independent group formed, led by a woman who was a longtime supporter of the police and a man who owned a bowling equipment store. They received strong support from the union that represented our police officers. Their primary funding base was small businesses in Springfield. They put together a proposal to amend the Springfield city charter. That proposal called for a property tax to add 24 new police officers but required the city to maintain 100 officers from other funds. The net result was to require the city to maintain a police department of 124 officers as well as the already required 127 firefighters. This provision arose from the fear that the city would use the new tax money to employ current officers rather than to add new officers. While the city manager had doubts about this kind of restriction on his administrative flexibility, the city commission concluded that it was a price we needed to pay in order to get the police officers we needed. The levy passed. Are 124 police officers enough for Springfield? That is always very difficult to answer. What is clear is that 124 police officers can provide much more police response than 89 can.

COMMUNITY ORIENTED POLICING

It is hard to imagine modern police work without the 911 system. In the case of an emergency—and at all too many other times, too—citizens dial 911. A dispatcher answers and gathers information. On the basis of that information, the dispatcher radios emergency personnel to respond to the situation. When it works well, it provides quick response and the proper personnel to deal with whatever led to the call. No one wants to get rid of this efficient 911 system, but in one community after another, police departments have concluded that it has created distance between the police and the people. The answer proposed usually goes by the name of community oriented policing.

In the early 1990s, assisted by a veteran Boston cop, the leadership of our neighborhoods, our police department leaders, and other city officials (including city commissioners) devised our plan, Community Oriented Policing (COP).[1] The philosophy of community oriented policing is that by getting to know the community, police can identify the issues about which the people care the most. The police can then work with the community with positive action to solve problems before they cause 911 calls. Often, the root problems identified are not what usually pass for police responsibility: boarded-up homes that are hangouts or traffic patterns that encourage speeding. The solutions may fall to other parts of city government or to groups outside of city government, which means that other people in city government need to be willing to cut through red tape to help the COP officers gain the confidence of the community. It also requires the

COP officers to get to know what resources there are outside of city government that can help address the community's issues. Most of all, it requires officers to step out of their cars, disconnect from the 911 system to some extent, and get to know the neighborhoods again.

Since this was a pilot project, it was targeted to a limited area, but targeting services is always a problem. If we spread a service across the whole city, it may not be concentrated enough to see results. If a service is not available to every neighborhood, those people who are left out feel cheated. In this case, every neighborhood wanted more police presence. The original plan was to work in a neighborhood for a year or two, solve some key issues, and move on to other neighborhoods. The assumption was that the COP officers would leave behind stable neighborhoods with good relations to the police, a well-functioning neighborhood association, and knowledge of how to solve their own problems. I was always doubtful that it would be that easy if the neighborhood had serious problems. This approach worked pretty well in one of the original neighborhoods, but not so well in the other. After two years we moved on to two new neighborhoods.

One of the neighborhoods chosen for the second round of COP emphasis was Westwatch. It became the greatest success story of COP in Springfield. U.S. 40 runs east/west through the middle of Springfield. Westwatch was the neighborhood on the Westside that ran parallel to U.S. 40 to its north. The areas farthest from downtown remain stable and middle-income with generally well-kept yards and the typical neighborhood problems, but the areas closer to downtown were changing. Middle-income homeowners were moving out or dying; rentals were increasing. The average income of the area relative to other neighborhoods in Springfield was declining. Many of the younger and generally poorer families moving in had more children, some of whom were troublesome teens. The teens of some families in the neighborhood who always had been in trouble joined with these new teens to form gangs. The presence of these gangs was immediately visible in the form of graffiti, a symptom of the deeper neighborhood changes that brought Westwatch neighbors to the police for help.

Two female officers were assigned to Westwatch, whose key leadership was also two women. Maybe that is why it worked so well. The two officers worked closely with the emerging Westwatch neighborhood association. One of the two key leaders moved out of the neighborhood but stayed involved at a different level. The other took over prime leadership. The COP officers came to know the neighborhood well and gained people's confidence. Westwatch began to learn how to use the city's system to address nuisance and housing code complaints. Westwatch contacts played a role in breaking up the Westside gangs, along with some gang violence and subsequent arrests of key gang leadership. Nuisance abatement (trash, weeds, structures in bad repair, etc.) resulted from increased city enforcement and from Westwatch threatening to turn people in to the city. Neighborhood cleanup days with trash dumpsters supplied by the city and a yearly Crime Night Out with music, food, door prizes, and entertainment in the middle of a street closed for the night were great successes. Most of all, many people in the Westwatch area who had just about given up gained new hope that they could make their neighborhood livable again.

Perhaps because of its great success, Westwatch became the big test of the COP philosophy. A new police chief always has new ideas. Named chief in November 1997, David Walters had been a captain during our discussion of the philosophy of COP. He had bought into the concept that COP should be a characteristic of the way policing is delivered all over the city, not a program for a few neighborhoods. He set out to devise a way of going citywide with COP, calling it "beat policing." The president of Westwatch rightly perceived that it would be a problem for Westwatch. The police officers who had been working with Westwatch would now be resource people citywide. There was no way that this would not reduce police presence in the Westwatch area. I appreciated Westwatch's point of view and thought they might be right. However, it was hard to deny that they had been getting more than their fair share of police service. The chief promised not to leave the old COP neighborhoods in the lurch, but he admitted he could not continue the service to which they had become accustomed.

STRUGGLING GENTRIFICATION

When Springfield was at the height of its prominence as an industrial power, the two places to live if you were wealthy were either South Fountain Avenue or East High Street. What remains of those glory days are some magnificent old mansions. In recent years, a subsidiary of the Turner Foundation has restored a number of homes on each street and put them up for sale. East High Street remains a relatively stable neighborhood, fighting to preserve its great homes but not known as an area of significant crime. South Fountain is different. In many ways, it is the primary location for testing the viability of diversity in Springfield today. A number of homes have been restored by Turner or by their owners, but they remain the minority. Most have not been restored significantly or are in some stage of deterioration. In addition, the side streets on either side of South Fountain are primarily relatively low-cost rentals. The entire time I have been on the Springfield City Commission, there has been drug activity on or near South Fountain. For a time we chase it to other places. But when we chase it out of those neighborhoods, it returns to South Fountain. Such is the battle with contemporary drug dealers that so frustrates urban police departments.

Most of the old-timers who have lived on South Fountain understand this reality. They do not accept it and ask for help when the problem worsens, but they understand that the city tries to address the problems. Some of the newcomers are not nearly as understanding. They want the drugs out of their neighborhood, and they do not want to hear excuses. One solution, the only real solution some urban experts would suggest, is for the neighborhood to change from its current mixed character to all middle- and upper-income homeowners. Most poor people are not drug dealers, but drug dealers can afford to work best when they are mixed into low-cost rentals. Most suburban and many of our better-off city neighborhoods are homogeneous, including few (if any) poor people. Due to major public and private investment, the neighborhood has fewer poor people now than it did ten years ago, but it will take much more investment to change the entire neighborhood. The end result would likely reduce crime in the neighborhood, but it would not provide the real diversity for which I have argued. Since the big investments that would be necessary are not likely to happen soon, South Fountain is more likely to be the most exciting neighborhood in town in both good and bad ways for some years to come.

RACE AND POLICE

Springfield also has had to deal with the police issue that scares urban politicians the most. In July 2002, a van left the road on South Yellow Springs Street and struck four young girls who were riding their bikes. One was injured very badly; she remains today in a nursing home. This tragedy is the greatest fear of every parent whose children go out to play. In this case the driver was a young white man, and the four girls were African American, raising additional issues. Hard as they looked, the Springfield police officers who investigated the accident could not find evidence of behavior by the driver that would support serious charges. Several reenactments of the accident did not suggest excessive speed. The blood test did not show impairment by alcohol and showed only a trace of marijuana, not enough to impair judgment. The county prosecutor concluded that there were not grounds for a felony charge.

The African American community of Springfield was irate. These events were tragic enough in their own right, but the failure to charge the driver with a felony added insult to injury. The common reaction was that, if a young black man did the same to four white girls, he would go away for a long time. Usually unstated was the history that most African Americans have had with police officers at some point in the past that leads them to assume the worst. Soon after this incident, a Springfield chapter of the Southern Christian Leadership Conference (SCLC) was formed. They led a march and started holding weekly rallies in support of the four girls, demanding tougher charges. When the SCLC group appeared at a city commission meeting, they were accompanied by a regional leader from Dayton, who threatened demonstrations and legal action. The vice president of the Springfield chapter of SCLC accused the police of not investigating the incident well enough and the city commission of ignoring the gap between the north and south of Springfield. For me, this cut very deeply. I believed that I had given a big piece of my life to closing that gap and hoped I had made a difference. One participant not speaking for SCLC threatened violence against the driver. I expressed the city commission's concern for the girls and its commitment to equal treatment, directed the police chief to work with the community, and urged citizens who had further information about the accident to report it to the police. I attended the next SCLC rally to repeat that and to pledge some of our family's personal money for a fund for the girl hurt the most.

At the time this all happened, the city already was in negotiation with a group of African American ministers about community relations. While that discussion initially had centered upon the hiring and promotion of African American police officers, it now broadened to police-community relations. Facilitated by the U.S. Department of Justice, these discussions produced a proposal for a Police Community Advisory Group (PCAG) to serve as a link between the police and the community. All the affected parties, including the police unions, agreed, and the city and the group of ministers signed a document laying out the purpose and structure of the group. As liaison, I recommended that the SCLC vice president, who had been so tough on the city commission, and a longtime local NAACP activist become members of the PCAG.

At its initial meeting, the PCAG agreed that its first big piece of business was to review the police investigation of the accident involving the four girls. After seeing all of the information, the group agreed unanimously that the police had done their job. Those with good contacts in the African American community said that the records showed that many of the rumors about what police had not done were untrue and that some of the signed statements by witnesses did not square with what these witnesses had told others in the community. By this time, some distance had developed between the local SCLC people and at least one of the families of the girls, and SCLC had backed off of the issue. The PCAG decided that it was better to just drop the matter than to reopen old wounds.

What this entire incident shows is that it is not sufficient to do the police work correctly. The police chief always believed that his officers had acted properly and tried hard to find out just what had happened. The record seems to bear that out. However, he dramatically underestimated how the well of suspicion of the police in the community could shape perceptions. Also, in his effort to protect the privacy of the families of the girls, he had left the public discussion open to rumors to which he did not respond quickly. As a city government, I think we learned that a little open communication with people trusted in the community can undercut misinformation. Hopefully, we are now better prepared to do that in the future with the help of the Police Community Advisory Group. Having said all of that, the relationship between a city's police and its citizens, especially its nonwhite citizens, remains a potential flash point for all American cities.

To our south, Cincinnati had been torn apart by incidents between the police and primarily young African American men. We now often forget that before 9/11 New York City had been similarly divided by such incidents. Then there was the Rodney King incident on the opposite coast. This clearly is a national challenge. If we had any doubts before, videotape now provides evidence that police have acted improperly in some cases that make the news. More common are the day-to-day or more often night-to-night encounters between police and citizens. Often, the citizens act in obnoxious and even dangerous ways, but we also know that police sometimes overreact. City government must be on guard to train our officers to act properly and to discipline officers we find to have acted improperly. At least as important, we need to build relationships that will allow us hear from the public and be heard. At the end of the day we also need to recognize the history and lack of hope that fuel suspicions of government officials and undermine confidence that justice will be done. I could not argue that there were no gaps between the various parts of our city or claim that I had been completely successful in closing them. This is as hard as the job of an urban politician gets.

ONGOING CHALLENGE

Like most cities, Springfield was a safer place to be in 2000 than it was in 1990. We added a bicycle patrol and then also expanded that much more broadly within the police department. A better city budget allowed us to restore crime prevention programs like Drug and Alcohol Resistance Education (DARE). The number of authorized positions in the police department reached a peak of 133, some funded by grants and some from the city's general fund. A number of our most violent residents were among those in prison, but they would almost all be out again. Surely, the growing economy helped a lot. A tight job market forced employers to hire even those who had trouble with the law in the past. While all of these conditions existed, more police officers closer to the people made a difference.

Then along came the recession of 2000–2004, which hit particularly hard in Ohio and especially in industrial cities like Springfield. We cut everything but personnel immediately and then began not filling vacancies. For a couple of years we exempted public safety forces from these cuts, but in time we had to leave vacancies unfilled in police and fire also. From the high of 133 authorized positions, police staffing declined down to the mandated level of 124. The clearest example of the effect of this reduction is another community relations program. In the spring of 2003, the drug dealers in a couple of our low-income neighborhoods became particularly brazen. The newspaper did a story composed mostly of interviews with residents of these neighborhoods about their fears for their safety and that of their children. At the next meeting of the city commission, Rev. Larry Coleman, later to add spirit to our successful All-America City effort, appeared. He spoke of the problems for members of his church and their neighbors created by the street crime and challenged us to do something. At least as importantly, he promised to work with the addicts and prostitutes (most of whom were also addicts) to try to turn their lives around. In cooperation with the courts, he set up a diversion program. At about the same time, JAM (Justice, Action and Mercy) urged the city to cooperate with their "hot spots" program. JAM is a political action program of a number of churches in Springfield. The hot spots program allowed people to fill out a card providing anonymous tips about crime. The police chief agreed to cooperate.

A major effort of the police department to work with these two citizen efforts was a street crime task force that operated during the summers of 2003 and 2004. It resulted in a large number of arrests and moved most street crime from residential neighborhoods to areas easier to control. At least it put the people that neighborhoods object to the most on the defensive. With the staff reductions forced by budget cuts, the police chief decided that it would be difficult to field the task force at the same level after 2004. The police tried to use their regular efforts to address the same problems, but they surely lost some momentum. The number of police officers available makes a difference to the livability of neighborhoods, and more police requires money. Clearly, good jobs and the hope they provide help reduce crime. Reducing the concentration of poverty would also help. There is a need for much more drug and alcohol treatment capacity. For now, police departments continue to try new things as well as do the old ones better. All central cities know all of this and are all trying something like what Springfield has done to provide safety to their citizens.

THE THIRD *S*: SCHOOLS

Space draws people to the suburbs; concerns over safety drive them there. However, middle-class Americans believe in nothing more than they believe in the value of education. In today's economy that insight is better grounded than ever before. Schools loom as the biggest *S*, driving those who can afford it to move to the suburbs. Urban schools are also the reality that strikes most clearly at the core of America's claim to believe in equal opportunity. Most Americans believe that every American child should have access to a good education. However, most of us do not understand the price that will cost or do not appear to be willing to pay that price.

At least once a year the front page of the *Springfield News-Sun*, Springfield's only newspaper, features the results of the latest Ohio proficiency scores. The unstated assumption is that these scores tell us how good a job of educating children each individual school and each school district is doing. For days afterward, local media feature criticism of the leadership of Springfield City Schools because their scores are much lower than the suburban schools. For anyone familiar with the neighborhoods of Springfield and where schools are located, a trend emerges with a closer look at the data. According to these test scores and the popular opinion, the schools our children attended—Highlands Elementary School, Hayward Middle School, and South High School—were "bad" schools. As the *Updating the Dream*[2] data indicated, these and the other schools reflect their neighborhoods. The average income of the neighborhood and the amount of poverty told us in a rough way how the schools compared in terms of their relative scores on tests. They also told us how likely students were to experience disruption in the classroom. Urban education is not for the fainthearted.

My primary political activity prior to joining the Springfield City Commission was working for levy campaigns for Springfield City Schools. Because of a state law that does not allow school districts to collect more revenue when property values go up, Ohio schools cannot keep pace with inflation, which means that they are constantly on the ballot for increases in local property taxes. As a result, I worked on many school levies; while I remained supportive of levies after I joined the city commission, my primary political efforts were aimed at two realities: tax base and state funding.

SCHOOL TAX BASE

Ohio public schools depend primarily upon property taxes for local support of schools. Each local school district decides, mostly by vote of the people, what rate (percentage) to charge itself for its schools. This is often called millage, because it is usually stated in terms of mils (one-tenth of 1 percent). The amount of local property tax a school district has to work with depends upon how much its property is worth and how high a percentage it charges itself. As far as local school funding is concerned, the value of the property a district may tax is its wealth. However, it makes a difference how many students that district needs to educate, so the figure usually used to compare how well off one district is compared to another is wealth per pupil. The table that follows lists these figures for Clark County school districts. According to the state of Ohio,[3] Springfield Shawnee (previously called Springfield Local) is by far the wealthiest district in Clark County, and Springfield City is the least wealthy. In 2004, Springfield Shawnee's wealth per pupil was $150,942, higher than the average of $129,497 for the state of Ohio. That is over 200 percent of Springfield City's $74,527 per pupil. Finally, the table shows how the wealth per pupil has changed in recent years. Specifically, it shows the change between 1987 and 2004; Springfield City started out behind but fell even further behind. In fact, Springfield City is the only district in the county whose wealth per pupil grew more slowly than the state average. This difference between the wealth of suburban and city schools is common around the country.

Ohio law adds another twist to this local school finance story. Annexation to a city in Ohio is totally a local process, primarily in the hands of the landowners who usually can annex to a city if they want to do so. School annexation, however, must be approved by the Ohio State Board of Education in a process entirely separate from municipal annexation and typically has been difficult. Cities like Columbus or Akron or Springfield are able to annex new suburban tax base; their respective city schools, however, usually are not. For instance, only a few areas have asked to join the Springfield City Schools. In Rusk's terms, these cities are much more elastic than their school systems are. In parts of the country such as the South, where school districts are broader (often countywide), they are much more elastic. This has had a very significant impact upon Springfield

Table 8.1. Comparison of Wealth per Pupil
for Clark County Schools in 1987 and 2004

District	1987 Wealth per Pupil	1987 State Wealth, Rank	2004 Wealth per Pupil	2004 State Wealth, Rank	Increase in Wealth 1987–2004
Mad River Green	$38,789	123	$122,461	233	316% (90%)[4]
Northeastern	$47,878	128	$119,716	246	250% (51%)
Northwestern	$46,552	173	$108,695	296	233% (41%)
Southeastern	$42,197	374	$107,040	308	254% (53%)
Springfield City	$35,428	339	$74,527	527	210% (27%)
Springfield Shawnee	$50,993	143	$150,942	138	296% (78%)
State of Ohio	$59,980		$129,497	(612 districts)	216% (30%)

City Schools. Nearly all of the school taxes paid from PrimeOhio industrial park and the North Bechtle commercial development went to Springfield Shawnee Schools (Springfield Township), not to Springfield City Schools. At the time of the Wittenberg study in 1996, this was a little less than $1 million a year; by 2005, it was more than $3 million a year. These two economic developments were the key increases in the city's tax base; Springfield City Schools missed out on both of them. One reason that it has fallen further behind other local districts is because Springfield City School District is inelastic. It is unable to include growth on the edge of the city within its district.

Because Springfield City has less wealth per pupil, it has to tax itself at a higher rate than Springfield Shawnee just to get the same amount of money per pupil from local property taxes. For instance, if each had taxed itself at 30 mils in 2004, Springfield Shawnee would have received $4,528 per pupil compared to the $2,235 Springfield City would have received, a $2,293-per-pupil advantage in local funds. One result is that Springfield City is much more dependent on federal and especially on state funds to meet the needs of its students, which makes it more vulnerable to the ups and downs of federal and state budgets. Another result of this inequality in tax base is that Springfield City Schools has to ask its voters to tax themselves at a higher rate in order to make up for a weaker tax base. The census data show that those voters, on average, have lower incomes from which to pay those higher tax rates. Small wonder that Springfield City Schools ran levies so often or that their voters became reluctant to pass them. The significance of this point is magnified by the fact that Springfield City Schools is attempting to educate a high proportion of children from lower-income families. This is a very difficult task, requiring greater resources than educating children from families with more income. Springfield City Schools has been unable to get these resources locally from growth in its tax base. In sum, our urban district faces the very difficult task of educating low-income children, but it has the least local resources in the area for doing that job. This situation certainly is not unique to Springfield or Ohio.

One solution to this tax-base problem would be for the tax base the city has annexed also to be annexed to the Springfield City School District. Under Ohio state law, however, this is unlikely. That leaves the possibility of some sort of revenue sharing between suburban schools and Springfield City Schools. The original draft of the CEDA agreement included revenue sharing between Springfield Shawnee School District and Springfield City Schools as the price for including Shawnee in the agreement, which would have meant that they could receive city utilities for their school buildings without annexing those buildings to the city. Springfield Shawnee turned down that deal. At the time, an Ohio Environmental Protection Agency employee said that it was likely that if public utility service was available near a Springfield Shawnee building, the Ohio EPA was likely to order them to hook up. The Southern Interceptor Sewer now runs right in front of Springfield Shawnee High School.

In other words, we might have been able to require Springfield Shawnee to join the CEDA agreement by sharing revenue with Springfield City Schools before providing them with utility service. In light of this, I suggested privately to the superintendent of Springfield Shawnee that it might be best to negotiate an agreement before we reached a crisis. When we met with representatives of Springfield City Schools, their finance person surprised us by not being very enthusiastic about revenue sharing. He explained that since the state of Ohio provides more state money to schools with lower tax bases, the state would cut the state grant to city schools a lot more than they would increase the state grant to Springfield Shawnee. As a result, Springfield Shawnee would lose a lot more than city schools would gain. At the same time, changes in state and federal law meant that the larger financial problem for Springfield City Schools was the transfer of pupils to suburban schools. Representatives of the city, including me, met with representatives of Springfield Shawnee to explore possibilities. That first meeting did not go well. Further discussions more than a year later went better. Springfield City Schools was focused upon loss of students, and Springfield Shawnee schools were full and their taxpayers were refusing to vote money to build new space. An agreement was reached that included a commitment by Springfield Shawnee not to accept any more out-of-district students and not to seek the city's income taxes in place of property tax rebates to attract businesses. The city agreed to extend needed utility service. A planner might have wanted the city to hold out for more, but the pluralists who have to work with other public officials compromised.

LOCAL FUNDING FOR SCHOOLS

In recent years, Ohio has become famous for more than football. The Supreme Court of Ohio has ruled four times that the state's way of funding schools is unconstitutional. The constitution calls for the adequate and equitable funding of schools by the state. The Supreme Court of Ohio found that, by depending too much on local property taxes to support public schools, the state was failing to provide adequate and equitable funding. However, the Supreme Court never clearly ordered the State General Assembly to enact any specific remedy, and changes in the makeup of the Supreme Court in the two most recent elections now make such an order unlikely. The General Assembly responded with a program for building public school facilities with a lot of state funding. However, it has not made much in new operating funds available to address directly the dependence on the local property tax.

In Springfield, the facilities program offered to pay 82 percent of the cost of rebuilding our public schools; a local property tax bond issue to fund the other 18 percent passed in Springfield. The state commission overseeing this program established the rule that if it costs more than two-thirds of the cost of a new building to renovate an old building, local districts must build new to get the state money. The same commission determined that all of Springfield's elementary and middle schools must be built new. Thirteen elementary schools were replaced by ten new ones; five middle schools were replaced by four new ones. That left the high schools, North and South. Initially, the state approved the renovation of South and construction of a new North. That was the plan when local voters approved the building bond issue. Later, more asbestos turned up, and it was decided that South should not be renovated. At that point, the Board of Education made a heroic decision.

North High School and South High School embody the social divisions of Springfield. Unlike most cities in the United States, Springfield does not have an affluent suburb. Both the wealthiest and the poorest neighborhoods in Clark County have existed inside the city. In part, this has been possible because the best elementary schools, Snowhill and Simon Kenton, serve affluent Springfield. The students from these two elementary schools went on to Roosevelt Middle School and North High School, where they had relatively little contact with the diversity our kids knew at Highlands Elementary School, Hayward Middle School, and South High School. This led Springfield North to have the strongest college preparatory program of any high school in the county. It also meant that Springfield had a large number of students doing well on the Scholastic Aptitude Test (SAT) as well as a large number of high school dropouts.

Some of the perceived differences between North and South were not real. According to the statistics reported to the Ohio Department of Education[5] for the 2003–4 school year, South was 51.9 percent white, 42.5 percent African American, and 48.4 percent economically disadvantaged, while North was 77.4 percent white, 19.9 percent African American, and 30.3 percent economically disadvantaged. North students did better on the ninth-grade state proficiency tests than did South students—but not by all that much. Still, the widely held view in Springfield was that North was the rich, white, academically strong high school and South was the poor, black, academically weak one. When changes in federal and state regulations made it possible for students living in the South district to attend North, many did, thus reducing the enrollment at South, especially in college preparatory courses. It became increasingly impossible to field the full range of such courses at South, undercutting the claim that South and North were offering comparable educational opportunities. In other words, perceptions led people to act in ways that made the perceptions more true each year. By 2004, it simply made sense to merge the two high schools. Given the evidence that students do better with the personal contact of a small school, the concept was one Springfield High School of around two thousand students, divided into four smaller learning communities.

When the state of Ohio found itself with budget problems between 2000 and 2005, it cut funding for day-to-day school operations. This, plus big increases for health insurance and the loss of students, forced Ohio school districts, especially urban ones, to the ballot for new local property tax levies. Springfield City Schools placed a levy on the ballot; it failed. They made significant cuts and put a new levy on the ballot; it also failed.

At this point, it was time to decide where the new high school was to be located. The Board of Education appointed a blue-ribbon committee to recommend a location. Many on the committee thought South, the former Springfield High School building, was the best site, but the official cost estimates showed North to be less expensive. Not discussed publicly was the suspicion that a South site added to merger would produce more white and middle-class flight from Springfield City Schools. After months of confusing debate, mostly over cost estimates, the committee split down the middle with one abstention. The Board of Education then voted to build the new high school on the North site.

Having alienated mostly Northsiders by merging the high schools and mostly Southsiders by locating the new high school at North and taking the fall for the inaction of the Ohio General Assembly, Springfield City Schools now faced a deep financial crisis. When the next levy failed, they had to borrow from the state, leading to financial oversight by the state. A new levy featuring the best-financed campaign ever also failed in November 2005, this time by around five hundred votes. The Board of Education had no choice but to ask people to vote again on a property tax levy in February 2006. The Board of Education increased the stakes significantly by announcing that if this levy failed, they would eliminate all extracurricular activities, including athletics. Congressman Dave Hobson and I had recorded a joint automated phone message. A Wittenberg education professor got his Sociology of Education class to help with the levy. As I described earlier, three African American ministers organized three prayer meetings for passage of the levy. Clara and a parent from her school organized elementary school parents to register other parents and get them to the polls. Students, especially those in high school, and their parents became involved as never before. The final vote was 58 percent to 42 percent, a very solid victory. It would be nice if the key was prayer, but the cynics suspected that threatening football was closer to God in Ohio.

Taken together, the decision to merge high schools and the deep financial difficulties are the reverse of what is needed to keep middle- and upper-income people in Springfield. In other cities, these kinds of developments generally have produced flight to suburban schools. Is there any reason to believe that the same will not happen here? Our greatest hope is that our suburban schools are not clearly better than Springfield City Schools, especially in college preparatory education. They also are struggling financially, so they have limited capacity to absorb new students. Springfield City Schools also is the only district in the county approved for the International Baccalaureate program, an externally reviewed college prep program recognized as superior. Having said that, the question before us is not even whether our citizens will embrace diversity. It is whether they will tolerate diversity within schools that provide the best education in our county for kids headed to college. Snowhill Elementary or Simon Kenton Elementary schools, Roosevelt Middle School, and the college prep track at Springfield High School will continue to provide an excellent path to college. Will people follow it if it involves greater diversity than ever before? Will they count diversity as one of the factors that goes into being a good school? Experience from other cities is not encouraging. Given the choice, Americans generally have turned their backs on diversity in favor of homogeneous schools in the suburbs. Time will tell if that pattern is duplicated in Springfield.

STATE SCHOOL FUNDING

In the midst of these developments I received a call from the United States Conference of Mayors. They had decided that mayors could not stand on the sidelines while states withdrew funding from urban education. Partly because Ohio was well known for ignoring the decisions of its Supreme Court, the conference chose to begin a program of mayoral involvement in school funding in Ohio. The mayors of the six largest cities in Ohio met once and decided to invite the mayors of the other cities over fifty thousand in population to join them. Thus began a process of education and action aimed at producing a campaign to bypass the legislature and go directly to the voters with a referendum to increase state funding for public schools and focus it upon districts with high numbers of special-needs students, including low-income ones. This sounds much easier to organize than it is.

The first problem is that the school funding formula is not a simple policy with clear and consistent principles. Rather, it is a political document resulting from many political compromises over decades. Every time we added new participants to the discussion, we went through another presentation explaining the present system. That was painful, and I came to believe it was a hurdle to action. The problem became even more complicated when the mayors sought to reach out to the major players in the funding of education in Ohio. The mayors pulled together several educational reform groups, including one that had already started a petition drive, and the standard professional groups, such as the associations of school boards, administrators and finance officers, and various teacher organizations. These groups represented very different interests and had histories of past antagonisms. Two stress cracks in any possible coalition became clear. First, some of these groups represent particular kinds of school districts. For example, the mayors represented urban districts with significant numbers of low-income students. Other groups represent a much broader group of districts with very different amounts of resources for funding schools and were trying to keep all of these various kinds of districts happy. Second, some of the participants wanted total reform based upon some pure principles. Others suspected that less systematic reforms had a better chance of success. I was crystal clear about my interest: I wanted more money for Springfield City Schools. I was very comfortable believing that this was a just interest because Springfield City has a low tax base per pupil and has a high percentage of low-income students. These are exactly the grounds upon which the Ohio Supreme Court ruled that the current system was unacceptable under the Ohio constitution.

The best solution to fundamental problems of urban education is dispersing the poor. Studies show that low-income children learn better in schools where most of the students come from middle- and upper-income families. Spreading the poor out can be done by making our suburbs more diverse with something like the MPDU program in Montgomery County, Maryland, or by providing vouchers to low-income students so they can attend suburban schools. I assume suburban parents would object to either of those solutions. If that is the case, and if we still think urban children should not be left behind, then we are going to have to be willing to commit the effort and money necessary to make urban schools work. A part of any effort to leave no child behind will be spending more state and federal money drawn significantly from suburban taxpayers on urban (and rural) education. In Ohio at least, elected officials thus far have failed to face that reality.

That was the elephant in the room of our mayors' discussions that no one wanted to address directly. In order to provide an adequate education for students in districts with low property value per pupil (mostly urban and rural districts), the state either must take away some of the money currently going to districts with high property value per pupil (mostly suburban) or increase the total amount of state money spent on education funding so that no districts are cut. In order to spend more money on education, the state of Ohio would need to raise some state tax. The education groups that joined our mayors' group opted for this solution, producing a proposal that would have the state Board of Education establish what it would cost to educate Ohio students and then require the legislature to fund that amount. They were not able to gather enough signatures to put this on the ballot in November 2007. With the election of a new Democratic governor in 2006 who promised to deal with school funding, the mayors preferred to give him time to come up with a plan.

BE CAREFUL, POLITICIANS

Finally, I feel duty bound as the husband of an outstanding kindergarten teacher to add a few words of caution to us politicians. America's colleges and universities are the finest in the world. There may be a number of reasons for that, but as a college professor I believe the key reason is that I and other college professors decide what to teach and how to teach it in our classrooms. I firmly believe that the secret of good education is to hire good teachers and then let them teach. Most politicians these days do not seem to believe that. Instead, in the name of accountability they pass laws that enable bureaucrats to add one requirement after another aimed at making bad teachers better. They pass laws that seek to identify successful and unsuccessful schools through constant standardized testing. The primary result of all of this testing is to label schools that serve more low-income kids failures and schools that serve more affluent kids successes. Then, the laws punish the schools that are labeled failures by enabling their most capable children to move to other schools.

Clara must show how everything she teaches meets state-established courses of instruction that fit the standardized tests. Educational bureaucrats call this "aligning the curriculum"; I call it "teaching to the test." Each year Clara goes through the local paper, looking through the lists of graduating seniors for the names of her former kindergarten kids. Then she looks up their addresses and sends them cards and a copy of what they told her the last day of kindergarten were their favorite things they had done in kindergarten. Some of the students respond to her cards and mention their best memories from kindergarten. Almost all of them mention things Clara no longer does because they do not fit with the tests.

On average, American students do not score as well as students in other countries, especially in Asia, on tests that measure memory of specific data or performance of standard procedures. In part, America's scores are held down by the inequalities built into our school system that I have discussed in this chapter. What American students do excel at in comparison with students from other countries is creativity and flexibility of thought. Which of our standardized tests measures those two traits well? Could it be that we are in danger of losing the very strength of our educational system by teaching to the test? I remain convinced that the two primary keys to educational success, especially in cities, are equal opportunity and good teachers. We either must disperse low-income kids throughout our schools or spend a lot more money on schools that serve low-income children than those that serve affluent children. At the same time, we need to hire capable teachers, compensate them appropriately, and leave them free to teach.

I am convinced that safety and schools are the most important factors to both the survival of cities and any hopes of attracting middle- and upper-income people back to those cities. They are usually the two leading reasons people give for moving out of cities. Neither is likely to be solved completely any time soon.

However, people need to believe that cities are safe enough and city schools are good enough that they can consider the appeal of diversity. Otherwise, cities will remain or more likely become even more home primarily to low-income people with disastrous results for those people and for our cities, for metropolitan areas and for our society. These are critical elements to any hopes of addressing the injustice that defines our contemporary metropolitan areas.

Chapter 9

Catching the Spirit
of Public Life

Several years ago, in an attempt to help students get a better sense of Springfield, I split my class into six groups. These groups visited various places of worship in Springfield and reported back to the class. I asked the students to choose a place different from what they already knew. At the end of the group report about one of our downtown establishment churches, I asked if anyone in the group had anything to add. A Pentecostal African American student from Cincinnati smiled and said, "You know the furniture is really nice, but I'm not sure you could catch the Spirit there." I cannot speak personally about the presence of the Spirit at that church; I suspect they can defend themselves quite well. What I do claim is that in spite of what all too many people may think, you can catch the Spirit at City Hall and in those other places where people act publicly. To understand that claim, we first must be clear about what I mean by public life.

PRINCIPLES OF PUBLIC LIFE

First, public life forces us to deal with the right to participate. We in government, and I think especially local government, dare not act without people having a genuine opportunity to express their opinions and to have those opinions taken seriously. If we do, they will let us know very directly; my number is in the phone book, and I buy groceries locally. As a result, we in public life learn to respect the right of people to participate in decisions that affect them. Sometimes that is very messy; often it takes more time than those from the private sector would like. Sometimes that is because we are too bureaucratic, but more often it is because we must take the time to let people have their say and to listen and to respond if we can.

There is no single thing that those addicts of our televised city commission meetings say to me more than to ask if we can not shut up our "regulars." Our law director has always been clear that the price we pay for letting any citizen speak who wants is letting our "regulars" talk. Our regulars represent a fundamental reality of public life; every citizen has the right to appear in the public debate. That is why our city commission has encouraged the expansion of organized neighborhood associations from three or four to around forty. Neighborhood associations provide the opportunity for people to have voices in the public arena. I believe that at its best one of the things we learn from public life is a respect for the right of others to a public life. In the final analysis, I believe this right is based in a spiritual commitment to the integrity of other human beings. We all are endowed by the same Creator with that integrity.

Second, public life forces us to deal with the claims of distributive justice. Time after time we have to decide what the fairest and most just course of action is. Should we provide a tax break to get a business to locate in Springfield when those taxes would otherwise be paid to the Springfield City Schools, who surely need the money? If we provide the tax break, we will have more jobs, which this community needs so much. Those jobs will provide the income that makes possible so many other important things in people's lives. On the other hand, good schools are essential to the educated workforce that will attract good jobs to our community and make it possible for our people to make a better living. We can debate this issue for a long time. In the process, we would need to consider a lot more facts specific to a particular decision. What is clear is that whatever we decide, we have to consider what is the just thing to do. Public life at its best raises one issue of justice after another about which we must think and vote.

At a time when citizens see elected public service in an extremely negative light, I am arguing that elected officials struggle with the claims of justice far more than those who elect them. I have served with a number of members of the Springfield City Commission over the years. I have agreed with some nearly all of the time; I have disagreed with others some of the time. All of them always justified the positions they took as the fairest and most just, and nearly all of the time I thought they believed what they said. I believe that all elected officials think and talk about justice in their public life almost all of the time; I also think that most elected officials vote for what they believe is most just almost all of the time. Now that does not mean that we agree about what is just or that we are not influenced by selfish interests, but we do understand that public life forces us to deal with the claims of justice.

How many citizens in the course of their daily lives struggle with such claims for justice? For most of us our lives are consumed by the concerns of our personal life and work so that the claims of justice seldom appear on our radar or, perhaps better, computer screens. We pursue these concerns primarily on the basis of self-interest or the interests of those around us. At the same time, we do claim that we want politicians who are free from special interests. However, we then proceed to vote for the candidate who will best serve our own special interest. Certainly, few of us spend much time thinking about the claims of justice or trying to figure out what is the most just way to organize our lives together. I believe that most of us in public life do. As in the case of respect for the right of others to a public life, I believe this quest for a just society is at root an act of the Spirit. Recognizing the claims that our neighbors have on us is an integral part of our love of God. Indeed it is the visible, real way that we live out that love. It is a fundamental faith commitment.

Last, public life forces us to think about the good of the whole community. For so long, Springfield and Clark County were known as a battleground for local governments. For years, we had a city health department and a county health department that shared both a building and a health commissioner. However, the employees worked different hours, received different benefits, and enforced different regulations. Springfield and Clark County each had their own recreation program, and then there was an entirely separate county park district. Springfield had land for an industrial park near our airport but no way to finance its development or maintenance. What was in the news the most were the annexation battles between the city of Springfield and Springfield Township.

In recent years, we have formed a combined health district, a combined park and recreation district, a Joint Economic Development District (JEDD) with Green Township at the city's airport, and a Cooperative Economic Development Agreement with Springfield Township. Some of these are firsts in the state of Ohio. A number of public officials played key roles in ending these battles. The work of city staff was essential to our success. A number of public citizens helped make these things happen. What all shared was the capacity to see that the good of the entire community was at least as important as the interests of particular individuals or groups.

In each case, some people opposed these changes because of old antagonism or groundless fears, but there were also individuals and groups with legitimate interests that made looking at the big picture difficult. There were city health nurses who legitimately feared that merger would water down health services to city children. There were volunteers committed to historical reenactment in a county park who feared it would get lost in the bigger organization. There were employees at the Air National Guard base at the airport who did not want to pay the 1 percent tax on their wages. There were city residents concerned that the sewer line that came with the CEDA agreement would speed up suburbanization.

All of these concerns are real and at least somewhat legitimate enough that they needed to be addressed. What they had in common is that they looked at the issue from a particular point of view rather than from the perspective of what is good for the entire community.

Time and again, the city commission makes decisions that probably hurt the interests of some people in order to improve the quality of the whole. Sometimes it is an easy choice; sometimes it is a tough one. Sometimes we may conclude that the good gained by the entire community is not sufficient to justify the loss to some. However, I think it is clear that it is an integral part of our job as public officials to ask what is good for the entire community. Luckily we have others in this community in and out of public office who are willing to ask that same question. Once again, I believe that a concern for the common good finally is an act of the Spirit. It speaks to the quality of the world we share that limits or expands the possibilities for our lives together. It is another way we love.

AN ANGEL IN OUR LIVES

More than twenty years ago, Clara began the practice of inviting her kindergarten kids to trick or treat at our house on Halloween. One year, a family arrived with four boys. The oldest of the boys had been in Clara's class the year before, and the second was then her student. The mother was one of the best parent volunteers in Clara's classroom. Soon after that Halloween visit, the mother wrote Clara saying that she wanted us to raise her children. I thought she was kidding. Within a year, a little sister was born. That is right, there were four boys and a girl all under six years of age. Over the nearly twenty years since, we sheltered the mother and kids from the father a number of times and kept the kids while the mother was in the mental health system and the father was absent or in jail. We developed a Christmas tradition of a lasagna and gifts with this family and celebrated each child's birthday when possible. The kids still call Clara her school name, Mrs. Copeland, but I am Warren. Often they say we are their grandparents.

The baby girl born into that family was Angel. Through the years, she came to live with us a number of times. We became licensed foster parents so this was fully legal. The father demonstrated at our church one Easter, wrote to a number of public officials attacking me and making charges that led to an informal investigation by human services, and threatened my life more than once. As they grew older, all four boys got into legal trouble with juvenile authorities; we visited them in jail and treatment centers and kept one in our home for a time so he would not have to go to a state juvenile facility. At various times we provided money to all of the boys, sometimes in return for work. As adults, two of them have been adjudicated and served time in prison, so we provided the clothes they needed from their family and visited them.

Along the way the mother, a chain smoker, contracted lung cancer. The boys were older, but her last wish was that we raise her daughter. We became legal guardians for Angel, who came to live with us full-time as a teenager. Angel's eighth-grade year included volleyball and basketball and strong academic performance but also the slow death of her mother. We love Angel as much as either of our birth children or any of our grandchildren. However, I agree with the first reaction of most of our friends. We must be crazy: two sixty-year-olds taking on a teenager? It isn't as though living through the teenage years with our Scott and Karen was that much fun. Actually Angel has been easier so far.

THE GOODNESS OF PUBLIC LIFE

I know there always is risk in using yourself as an example, but I hope it brings an important issue alive. I understand the response of those who say, "You are such good Christian people to take this girl into your home." I think we are. But why do people seldom say we are just as good and Christian, if not more so, to give the time and effort we put into the public life of Springfield? Why is the direct relationship of a legal guardian so often seen as more of an act of faith than the principled participation in a community's public life? Our motivations for being legal guardians are mixed, just as our motivations for our public life are. Being legal guardians for a teenager is not significantly less complicated than being a good public citizen.

By the way, in what I have just written I did not intend to give Clara credit for being the good political wife. I saw her reaction to the local CBS station's coverage of my announcement that I was running for mayor—what she calls the "stand-by-your-man" coverage—well enough to know that that is not a role she seeks. At the time of that announcement, Clara was deeply involved in public life as the president of the board of directors of Project Woman, a shelter against abuse. Those who have served on the board of a voluntary association know that that can be just as difficult as government. Inasmuch as such voluntary associations shape our communities and understanding of the issues we face, they are actors in our public life. Public life takes many forms.

However, in our day trivial partisan politics has led many people to doubt whether human action should be public—let alone governmental. This has produced the paradox that students who enter my college classroom are more likely to have volunteered for some good cause than ever before and yet are no more likely to vote than earlier generations. They are convinced that they can love their neighbor one by one without paying attention to open housing laws and that they can build Habitat for Humanity homes and not worry about federal funds for public housing. It seems so much simpler, and the results seem so much more obvious. After taking a course from me, they usually understand an issue more deeply; I am less sure that they are convinced that public action can change things. I am least certain that very many of them go away believing that they can act publicly to change things.

Individuals should love their neighbors. If everyone did, there would be much less for city government to do. It is good that people volunteer to build houses, to tutor children, or to shelter the homeless. However, one year I voted to support the building of over two hundred units of new housing for low- and moderate-income families through various projects supported by a federal tax credit program. More recently, the HOPE VI grant seeks to change a whole neighborhood. Through housing or rent vouchers, our local public housing authority provides almost two thousand units of housing. After about twenty years of magnificent effort, our local chapter of Habitat for Humanity has built forty homes for people who needed them. Voluntary organizations provide a human touch and often a spiritual dimension that may be missing from government programs. However, we are not about to meet the huge needs of our urban communities through volunteerism. The decimal point is simply in the wrong place.

But there is a more fundamental reason that public action is necessary. Addressing many of the issues in our metropolitan areas requires change in the very structure of how we live our lives. Which schools most of our children attend, how they are funded, and how they are organized to teach cannot be decided by individual or voluntary efforts. These will require governmental solutions, hopefully informed by a concern for justice. People can attempt to solve their personal educational needs by pulling their children out of public schools or by moving to a community with public schools that seem to work well. Generally this only makes things worse for the vast majority of our children and makes the overall education system less just.

Government makes decisions that shape how an entire community operates according to some principles of justice. At each meeting of the Springfield City Commission, I vote on laws that imply some sense of what makes for a just society. I do not think that an elected official can do otherwise. I also try to act justly as an individual and support voluntary groups that advocate justice. Both are essential to a democratic society. Whether they recognize it or not, governmental bodies and elected officials inevitably face choices about the extent and character of justice in their communities.

THE REAL TEST OF FAITH

That brings me to the most profound issue of faith in my life. I believe that the fundamental values of real freedom and real diversity are essential to the experience of full humanity in our human communities. I believe that the ethical principles of respect for the integrity of other human beings, recognition of the just claims of our neighbors, and concern for the common good deserve our commitment. These are the values and beliefs that I seek to understand more fully and concretely and that I attempt to explain to my friends and students. Indeed, this has been the core of my professional academic life as a social ethicist. I find it intellectually stimulating and believe it is academically important. I also try to act inspired by these values and guided by these principles in both my private and public lives. I hold them very dear, and I want others to hold them just as dear as I do. However, they are not what most attracted me to public life or what holds me so tightly in it. And they are not the most fundamental faith issue I, and I believe we, face.

At each meeting of the Springfield City Commission, I vote on laws that have the potential to affect a number of my fellow citizens, to create greater or less justice, and to shape our entire community. I am able to vote, inspired by my fundamental values of freedom and diversity. I get to vote! Now, much of the time I am frustrated by federal and state limitations upon my capacity to freely decide for my community. I also am constantly aware that my decisions are restricted by what the market will allow and by what citizens will support. But I get to vote! I get to stand in the face of the apparent inevitability of the decline of industrial cities leaving so many people behind and of urban sprawl and the inequality and divisions it produces. And on the basis of my commitment to real freedom and real diversity, I get to vote! My faith is that by voting and through all of the other things I do in my public life, I actually am making history. Perhaps I am making just a little history, but I am making history. I am changing the course of human events if just a bit, and the changes I make create opportunities for other changes throughout future years.

Opportunities to act are not limited to serving as elected officials. I am not the only one who gets to vote. First, I am very aware that I would not be able to vote if it were not for the hundreds of people over the years who have volunteered in my campaigns or written checks to my campaign committee or voted for me. My favorite auto dealer gave innumerable hours to the work of developing industrial parks in Springfield and filling them with businesses that provide jobs for our citizens. Perhaps this allowed more people to buy cars from him, but not nearly enough to justify all of the time and effort he put in it. He changed the course of Springfield's history. The retired school secretary who has given endless hours to fight the deterioration of her Westside neighborhood and to develop a citywide association of neighborhood associations is just one of hundreds of neighborhood leaders who have changed the course of Springfield's history. The hundreds of citizens who participated in making something important of David Rusk's advice to Springfield changed the course of Springfield's history.

Each year we hold a celebration to recognize all the volunteers who serve on Springfield's city boards and committees in an effort to recognize their citizen action. In providing the first level of city government, they change the course of Springfield's history. Our entire effort at Community Oriented Policing required citizens committed to making their neighborhoods safer places to live. Some took significant personal risks, and many gave many hours to change the course of Springfield's history. The local members of the hospital board and the citizens who organized the Hospital Downtown campaign helped change the course of Springfield's history. The school levy committee, parent and student volunteers, Wittenberg education majors, pastors leading prayers, and the Chamber of Commerce all played important roles in passing a crucial school levy, and in the process they changed the course of Springfield's history.

Public action takes many forms and is done by many people. What all of the examples of public action that I have mentioned have in common is that people acted upon the situations in which they found themselves in ways that shifted the direction of subsequent events. Typically this action has greater effect when people act together with other citizens. In some cases, history is changed just a bit; in other cases, the long-term effects are more significant. In every case, the hopes that lead people to act and the courage that it takes to act confirm my faith in the value of public action and inspire me to act in the faith that such action has meaning.

My deepest faith is that my action and that of my fellow citizens makes some difference. I have faith that God has entrusted us with the power to make history. As someone who meddles in social science, I have the capacity to make convincing arguments for the continuation of the status quo into the future, for an unbroken causal link between the past and the future. In fact, I spend a lot of time in my courses trying to help my students see that history does shape significantly the choices before us if we try to deal with racism or sexism or poverty or cities. It is easy to argue for historical determination. However, my faith is that the future is not totally determined. My faith is that inspired by the Spirit of Love, we can act in each moment so that the future is marked by real freedom and real diversity. In fact, I am convinced that action inspired by the Spirit of Love is a significant act of faith, even if there is little immediate evidence of success. Some might think that this is a naive faith, but I believe it is the faith at the core of the best of public action. The deepest fear I have is that it is a faith not shared deeply enough by my fellow citizens, especially by those who are also open at least partially to the claims of real freedom and real diversity.

I once sat in a graduate course in political science at the University of Chicago in which the professor stated that during the 1950s his discipline had developed magnificent analytic tools which allowed them to predict the vast majority of the political behavior of the 1960s and 1970s. Essentially, these analytic tools predicted that the future would be an extension of the past, that things would not change very much. But in fact, the future is shaped dramatically by the past, although most Americans doubt that or just do not find history interesting. He said that political scientists predicted the vast majority of what happened in the 1960s. All they missed was the civil rights movement, the antiwar movement, the environmental movement, and the women's movement. All they missed was the novelty that could not be predicted from the past. All they missed was the making of history. Too many of my students, past and present, cannot really imagine effective action to reduce poverty, racism, pollution, sexism, or sprawl in urban America. They do not believe that they can make history. They do not share my faith in action. As two of my teachers and friends put it in regard to race, "in America it is easier to believe in life beyond the grave than it is to believe in life beyond the color line."[1]

Those of us who came of age in the 1960s were profoundly lucky to have all around us examples of meaningful action. Sadly, we often still refer to those experiences or to South Africa's freedom struggle to illustrate the power of public action. It is past time that we made some new history to talk about in the future. On Martin Luther King Day, we seldom sing the song that expressed the faith of his movement "We shall overcome. . . . We shall overcome. . . . We shall overcome some day. Deep in my heart, I do believe . . . we shall overcome some day." It just seems too naive for those of us so sophisticated or jaded by subsequent events. Those who sang it and believed it indeed were naive, but they also made history.

I am convinced that today our cities are as good a place as any to take a stand in the midst of history for values worth our best, values like real freedom and real diversity. Cities remain the principal places where those values are at stake in American life. I firmly believe that we are not yet condemned to a life of separation into subdivisions of sameness, surrounding inner cities of despair, but I recognize that we are trending in that direction. Only committed public action can get in the way of what may seem to many to be inevitable. I am convinced that urban politics is one way to take a stand for those values, convinced enough to give a big chunk of my life to it.

By the end of the course I teach on social ethics and urban life, most of my students are convinced that the shape of our metropolitan areas is an ethical issue. They often are pretty sure that there are some policies that could make a difference, such as dispersing the poor into the suburbs or sharing revenue between affluent suburban school districts and struggling urban ones. What they are least optimistic about is the likelihood that a majority of average citizens, especially those living in more affluent areas, will support these policies. In a democracy, that is a serious problem. I encourage others to consider a life in urban politics, in or out of elected office, or a life of actively supporting those living such lives. However, the greatest need may well be for average citizens (and those in a position to influence them) to catch the Spirit for justice in our metropolitan areas. Making history requires action from many people doing what they can. That is what it will take for justice to grow in our cities. May the Spirit move us to take a stand for justice in our cities while we can.

Notes

Introduction

1. *Newsweek: Special Anniversary Issue*, Spring 1983.
2. Ibid., 145.
3. Warren R. Copeland, "Introduction," in *Issues of Justice*, ed. Roger D. Hatch and Warren R. Copeland (Macon, Ga.: Mercer University Press, 1988), 1–26, describes this approach to social ethics in greater detail.
4. Michael Gastner, Cosma Shalizi, and Mark Newman, "Maps and Cartograms of the 2004 US Presidential Election Results," http://www-personal.umich .edu/~mejn/election/2004/. This link also includes a link to the original *USA Today* map.
5. David Rusk, *Inside Game/Outside Game*, develops and illustrates this distinction between metropolitan solutions (outside game) solutions and city-only solutions (inside game) solutions.

Chapter 1: The Call

1. William A. Kinnison, *Springfield & Clark County: An Illustrated History* (Northridge, Calif.: Windore Publications, 1985), 13. Much of the description that follows is drawn from this source.
2. It was actually declared such by the National Association of Real Estate Exchanges in 1973.
3. Kinnison, *Springfield & Clark County*, 72–73.
4. Ibid., 111, and *Newsweek*, 145–46. This strike lasted six months, leaving scars that have yet fully healed.
5. Kinnison, *Springfield & Clark County*, 111 and *Newsweek*, 146.
6. *Newsweek*, 160.
7. Warren Copeland, *And the Poor Get Welfare* (Nashville: Abingdon Press, 1994).

Chapter 2: Rusk's Elasticity Stretches Springfield

1. David Rusk, *Cities without Suburbs*, 2nd ed. (Washington, D.C.: Woodrow Wilson Center Press, 1995).

2. "Updating the Dream: Springfield Looks at 2000 and Beyond," *Springfield News-Sun*, March 30, 1997, insert.
3. Rusk, *Cities without Suburbs*, 9–10.
4. William Julius Wilson, *The Truly Disadvantaged* (Chicago: University of Chicago Press, 1987).
5. What follows is my summary of the entire argument of *Cities without Suburbs*.
6. Rusk, *Cities without Suburbs*, Table A-2.
7. Most of the economic data presented here was pulled together by Jeff Ankrom for Jeff Ankrom and Warren Copeland, "Springfield/Clark County's Population and Economy," in *Updating the Dream*, available at http://www4.wittenberg.edu/academics/urban_studies/TABLCONT.html.
8. The following discussion is drawn from Ralph Lenz, "Housing in Springfield and Clark County," in *Updating the Dream*, available at http://www4.wittenberg.edu/academics/urban_studies/TABLCONT.html.
9. The 2000 data is from Jeff Ankrom, Olga Medvedkov, and Frederick Tiffany, "The Market for Housing in Springfield and Clark County," Report to the City of Springfield, 2002, available at http://www4.wittenberg.edu/academics/urban_studies/housingstudy.htm.
10. The following discussion is drawn from John R. Baker, "Political Fragmentation, Elasticity and Center-Fringe Conflict," in *Updating the Dream*, available at http://www4.wittenberg.edu/academics/urban_studies/TABLCONT.html.
11. John M. Orbell and Toru Uno, "A Theory of Neighborhood Problem Solving: Political Action vs. Residential Mobility," *American Political Science Review* 66, no. 2 (June 1972): 471–89.
12. Thomas R. Dye, "City-Suburban Social Distance and Public Policy," *Social Forces* 44, no. 1 (September 1965): 100–106.

Chapter 3: Wilson's Concentration of Poverty Divides Springfield

1. William Julius Wilson, *The Truly Disadvantaged* (Chicago: University of Chicago Press, 1987), 46–62.
2. The following discussion is drawn from Ralph Lenz, "Is Wilson's Analysis True of Springfield?" in *Updating the Dream*, available at http://www4.wittenberg.edu/academics/urban_studies/TABLCONT.html.
3. The census data was compiled by Jeff Ankrom for Jeff Ankrom and Warren Copeland, "A Tale of Census Tracts," in *Updating the Dream*, available at http://www4.wittenberg.edu/academics/urban_studies/TABLCONT.html.
4. Clifford Brown collected most of the data for Clifford Brown, Jeff Ankrom, and Warren Copeland, "Schools in Springfield and Clark County," in *Updating the Dream*, available at http://www4.wittenberg.edu/academics/urban_studies/TABLCONT.html. I added more recent data.
5. http://www.ode.state.oh.us/.
6. This is an estimate. For some reason, the state does not have a summary number for Emerson, but its scores on the various parts of the test are very close to Fulton's.
7. This discussion is drawn from David Nibert, "Crime in Springfield and Clark County," *Updating the Dream*, available at http://www4.wittenberg.edu/academics/urban_studies/TABLCONT.html.

Chapter 4: Four Ethical Angles on the City

1. Those familiar with Aristotle might recognize the four causes in what follows. I would associate the competitive city with the efficient cause, the populist

city with the material cause, the pluralist city with the formal cause and the planned city with the final cause.

2. Paul E. Peterson, *City Limits* (Chicago: University of Chicago Press, 1981), presents a classic statement of the competitive city position. Clarence N. Stone, *Regime Politics: Governing Atlanta, 1946–1988* (Lawrence: University Press of Kansas, 1989), is a critical view of this position.

3. Jeffrey M. Berry, Kent E. Portney and Ken Thomson, *The Rebirth of Urban Democracy* (Washington, D.C.: Brookings, 1993) offers a good expression of this perspective.

4. Robert A. Dahl, *Who Governs* (New Haven, Conn.: Yale University Press, 1961), is the classic example of the pluralist position related to city government. Paul Schumaker, *Critical Pluralism, Democratic Performance and Community Power* (Lawrence: University Press of Kansas, 1990), presents a more recent statement of this position.

5. David Rusk, *Inside Game/Outside Game* (Washington, D.C.: Brookings Institution Press, 1999), and Myron Orfield, *Metropolitics* (Washington, D.C.: Brookings Institution Press, 1997), are good expressions of this perspective. The entire Fall 2000 issue of *State and Local Government Review* also expresses this position.

Chapter 5: Living a Faith of the Prodigal Son and Good Samaritan

1. James Luther Adams, "The Love of God," in *On Being Human Religiously*, ed. Max L. Stackhouse (Boston: Beacon, 1976), 100.

2. Ibid., 97–99.

3. Matt. 25:31–46.

Chapter 6: Freedom and Diversity

1. Alfred North Whitehead, *Adventures of Ideas*, Free Press paperback edition (New York: Free Press, 1933).

2. Ibid., 95–96.

3. Ibid., 69–86.

4. Ibid., 69–70.

5. Ibid., 65–66.

6. Ibid., 66.

7. Douglas Sturm, "Introduction," in *Belonging Together*, ed. Douglas Sturm (Claremont, Calif.: P&F Press, 2003), 1–17, is an excellent Whiteheadian description of human experience especially as related to politics.

Chapter 7: The Three *A*'s for Creating Diverse Cities

1. This discussion is based upon David Rusk, *Inside Game/Outside Game* (Washington, D.C.: Brookings Institution Press, 1999), 178–200.

2. David Rusk, *Baltimore Unbound* (Baltimore, Md.: Johns Hopkins University Press, 1996).

3. Rusk, *Inside Game/Outside Game*, 191.

4. Myron Orfield, *Metropolitics: A Regional Agenda for Community and Stability* (Washington, D.C.: Brookings Institution Press and Cambridge, Mass.: The Lincoln Institute of Land Policy, 1997).

5. Rusk, *Inside Game/Outside Game*, 258–59.

6. Jeff Ankrom, Olga Medvedkov, and Frederick Tiffany, "The Market for Housing in Springfield and Clark County," Report to the City of Springfield,

2002, available at http://www4.wittenberg.edu/academics/urban_studies/ housingstudy.htm.

7. Rusk, *Inside Game/Outside Game*, 11–12.

Chapter 8: The Three *S*'s for Preserving Diverse Cities

1. The term "community oriented policing" does not belong to Springfield. It is a national movement that Bill Clinton picked up on in pushing legislation for more police on the street.

2. Clifford Brown, Jeff Ankrom, and Warren Copeland, "Schools in Springfield and Clark County," in *Updating the Dream*, available at http://www4 .wittenberg.edu/academics/urban_studies/TABLCONT.html.

3. The data that follows including that in Table 8 is most easily available from the Ohio Department of Taxation at http://www.tax.ohio.gov/divisions/tax_ analysis/tax_data_series/publications_tds_property.stm#AllPropertyTaxes.

4. The increases adjusted for inflation are in parentheses.

5. http://ilrc.ode.state.oh.us/Downloads.asp.

Chapter 9: Catching the Spirit of Public Life

1. Alan Anderson and George Pickering, *Confronting the Color Line* (Athens: University of Georgia Press, 1986), 396.

Index